SHINE LIKE A DIAMOND

Embracing The Process

By Lisa Dew

"Lisa has captured some beautiful truths in her new book "Shine like a diamond" that are not only inspiring but transforming to all who read these words. I have had the privilege of watching her journey of moving from a piece of coal to shining like a diamond herself. She is experienced in the business of heart change and heart exchange in an authentic way. I love how she is running her own race, set free from the trap of comparison and I know you will too. Filled with scripture and personal stories you will be greatly encouraged by her testimonies, insights and personal journey with God"!

— ROMA WATERMAN, FOUNDER
HEARTSONG PROPHETIC ALLIANCE
AWARD WINNING
SINGER/SONGWRITER, AUTHOR AND
WORSHIP LEADER.

"Having read "Shine Like a Diamond" at a time in my life when everything felt like a challenge, I have been inspired to dig deeper to try & find the diamond God has placed inside of me. I believe everyone could benefit from reading this book no matter what stage of life you are in or where you are in your walk with God. Everyone has burdens & struggles. This book is broad & versatile enough to apply to whatever your challenges. It is anointed & thought provoking! I highly recommend it."

— CAELA DE WITT

SCRIPTURE REFERENCES

- All scriptures marked (TPT) are used with permission from The Passion Translation. Copyright © 2017, 2018 by Passion and Fire Ministries, Inc. All rights reserved.
- All scriptures marked (AMP) are used with permission from the Amplified Bible. Copyright © 1954, 1958, 1962, 1964, 1965, 1987 by The Lockman Foundation.
- All scriptures marked (NIV) are used with permission from the Holy Bible, New International version. Copyright © 1973, 1978, 1984, 2011 by Biblica, Inc. All rights reserved.
- All scriptures marked (NLT) are used with permission from the Holy Bible, New Living Translation, copyright © 1996, 2004, 2015 by Tindal House Foundation. All rights reserved.
- All scriptures marked (MSG) are used with

permission of NavPress from THE MESSAGE, copyright © 1993, 2002, 2018 by Eugene H. Peterson. Represented by Tyndale House Publishers, a division of Tyndale House Ministries. All rights reserved.

Self published and printed by Lisa Dew - Auckland New Zealand.

Front cover and interior designed by Lisa Dew.

Copyright © 2022 by Lisa Dew

All rights reserved. This book or any portion thereof may not be reproduced or used in any manner whatsoever without the express written permission of Lisa Dew except for the use of brief quotations.

Website: www.lisadewcreations.com

ISBN: 978-0-473-64246-4 Soft Cover

ISBN: 978-0-473-64247-1 Soft Cover POD

CONTENTS

Introduction ix

Chapter 1 - Passion, Power, & Purpose	1
Chapter 2 - Proclamation & Praise	13
Chapter 3 - Pressure And Pain	39
Chapter 4 - Position And Perspective	59
Chapter 5 - Prayer And Prophecy	85
Chapter 6 - Patience And Perseverance	113
Chapter 7 - Protection And Preparation	127
A Word From Lisa	144

INTRODUCTION

There is almost always a delay between receiving a promise and taking possession of it. This delay or gap in time is where a process occurs. A promise is full of potential for something greater, but without going through the process, that potential for greatness will never be realised.

Diamonds are just rocks with potential, harvested from within the depths of the earth. You would never even know they were there if you didn't go digging for them, and even if you found one, it wouldn't look like much unless you really knew what you were looking for. Once discovered and brought to the surface, diamonds must then go through a rigorous process taking up to around five months before they are ready to be set as a stunning jewel on a piece of jewellery. We are like that diamond in the rough. Without God we are full of potential, but it may never be realised unless we submit to God, the 'master jeweller'. Submission doesn't always come easily. It happens as part of a process.

With diamonds, the process is long and meticulous. Once they have been sorted into categories according to their weight, colour, and clarity, experts then decide how the diamond should be cut in order to maximise its value and clarity. Cutting diamonds is a very specialised job that requires special tools, knowledge, and technique. A diamond can only be cut by another diamond. There are five steps in cutting a diamond. They are:

1. **Planning** – An expert will carefully plan how the diamond will be cut.
2. **Cleaving** – This is the process where diamonds are used to cut one diamond into multiple pieces.
3. **Bruiting** – This step is where the diamond is shaped into a specific cut. This process is the most intensive and takes the most time to perfect.
4. **Polishing** – Without the polishing phase, a diamond would be dull and not shine.
5. **Inspecting** – The last step in this process is the final inspection. An expert will use specific magnifying glasses to review its cut and value.

Fortunately, we don't have to go through this exact process to come out shining in the hands of "the master jeweller." God takes us through a different kind of process, but like a diamond, you and I have hidden potential. We are all going through a necessary yet often painful process to bring out the best in us. God is transforming us from glory to glory. In this book, I have given each of the elements involved within the process a label beginning with the letter 'P'. I have chosen to divide each chapter into two or more similar elements —all important components of the refining power of the process we need to go through in order to reach our full potential and come out shining. They are:

- Passion, Power, and Purpose
- Proclamation and Praise
- Pressure and Pain
- Position and Perspective
- Prayer and Prophecy
- Patience and Perseverance
- Protection and Preparation

Chapter 1

Passion, Power, & Purpose

There are two ways we can navigate this journey. We can try to do it in our own strength, clinging to control; stumbling along in the dark using our five physical senses, or we can pursue a refining, transforming, and life-changing relationship of intimacy with Holy Spirit.

When it was time for Jesus to leave us and ascend to Heaven, He left us an AMAZING GIFT. Holy Spirit, who never leaves us. He is a person. Not in the flesh as we are, but a person never the less. Learning to attune our spiritual eyes and ears to His promptings will empower us in our daily lives. He wants us to develop an ever deepening relationship with Him so that He can draw out the very best in us and help us to live this exciting adventure, serving God in what He has uniquely called us to.

HOLY SPIRIT is our most valuable resource. He is the source of everything we could ever need to navigate life. Don't try to do life in your own strength. Wisdom, knowledge, power, strength, purpose, systems and strategies, peace, joy, hope, healing—whatever we need, we must just ask Him.

CHAPTER 1 - PASSION, POWER, & PURPOSE

"Purpose is the reason you journey. Passion is the fire that lights the way."

— *AUTHOR UNKNOWN*

God wants us to live a life of passion, power, and purpose. But in order to live out our full potential we are going to have to learn some important lessons. The only way we are going to learn is by going through and embracing the transforming process that has been expertly designed and individually custom-made by God for us. He alone knows what we need in order to shine like a diamond in His expert hands.

Jesus is the ultimate example of a life of passion, power, and purpose, BUT his true calling or ministry didn't fully activate until He was thirty-three years old. That didn't mean that God didn't use Jesus in the meantime. That doesn't mean that Jesus had no purpose up to that point. There may have been a time in Jesus' life when on the surface, He was just a carpenter. In fact, it may have been quite a mundane job. Have you ever said, "I'm 'just a mother'"? I know I have. Oh boy, how we underestimate the importance of this role! Just because Jesus wasn't officially in ministry doesn't mean that He didn't have a destiny to fulfil nor that what He was doing wasn't useful. Like Jesus, God puts everything we do, even during those in between seasons, to good use. It's all part of the refining process. It's all preparation.

There was a time in my life when everything seemed bleak. I had a lot of dreams and ideas, but life was just mundane and ordinary. I had passion, but because I couldn't follow through on the things I was passionate about, I felt very little hope for the future. There were several scriptures during that time that helped keep me from becoming completely despondent. One of those was Proverbs 13:12. I particularly like the Passion Translation, which says, *"When hope's dream seems to drag on and on, the delay can be depressing. But when at last your dream comes true, life's sweetness will satisfy your soul."* I just had to hang in there and keep believing that that day would come. I will speak more about this in a further chapter. My point is that having passion without purpose can be miserable. I wholeheartedly believe that it is God who gives us meaningful purpose in life, and so it stands to reason that it is also God that places dreams and aspirations within our hearts. While my hope was deferred, I was sometimes guilty of feeling like God was somehow holding out on me— allowing me to feel the desire to do something meaningful whilst my life felt so meaningless! But as I pressed into God and learned to trust Him with my dreams, I realised that that simply wasn't the case. God was just waiting for the right time.

Without passion, we would not have the motivation to fulfil what God has called us to, nor the road map. What I mean by road map is that our passion reveals the path we should take. They are the signs along life's path that steer us in the right direction. Passion also helps us to have focus. The truth is that there are so many needs in the world—so many good things that we could do to serve the Kingdom, but we will burn out or simply spread ourselves too thin if we fall into the trap of thinking we have to do everything for everyone. No! That is not God's way. That is a lie of the enemy. If we try to be everything to everyone—serve every need that arises, we will end up not having the focus or energy to achieve anything of substance or importance. Passion has to have a channel. It must be focused in the right direction.

Passion can sometimes get out of hand. Take Saul, for example. Before he encountered God and received the name change to Paul, he was a very passionate man, but his zeal was misplaced until it came into alignment with God's will. (Philippians 3:6) Our emotions have the potential to lead us astray, but they are not evil; they just need to be submitted to the will of God. When we follow the promptings of our heart, we can be sure that we are moving towards the call of God in our lives. That is, let me be clear, if we are walking in close relationship with the Spirit and not just listening to the flesh.

It's well known that people are power- hungry. We can see many obvious examples throughout history right back as far as the days of Moses and beyond. Men like the Pharaohs of Egypt, and more recently names like Stalin and Hitler and now Putin stand out as men who are hungry for power. But this desire for power only seems to create death and destruction. That is not the kind of power God wants us to have. God's ideal is not for our passion and purpose to be for power, but rather for His power to be what fuels our passion and purpose. We can have all the passion and purpose we want, but without the power of God to 'fuel the fire' as it were, then our efforts would be futile. We need the fire of God in us to ignite our passion. Luke 3:16 (NLT) *"John answered their questions by saying, "I baptize you with water; but someone is coming soon who is greater than I am—so much greater that I'm not even worthy of being his slave and untying the straps of his sandals. He will baptize you with the Holy Spirit and with fire."* If we truly want to live a life pleasing to God, we must be filled with the spirit of God and with His fire. The fire of God is what gives us the boldness to fulfil the call of God. It stirs up a holy fervour in us. We cannot fully succeed in what God calls us to do with any lasting impact without it. The fire of God is evidence of His presence and anointing in our lives. 2 Chronicles 7:1-3 (NLT) *"When Solomon finished praying, fire flashed down from heaven and burned up the burnt offerings and sacrifices, and the glorious presence of the Lord filled the Temple. The priests could not enter the Temple of the Lord because the glorious presence of the Lord filled it. When all the people of Israel saw the fire coming down and the glorious presence of the Lord filling the Temple, they fell face down on the ground and worshiped and praised the Lord, saying, "He is good! His faithful love endures forever!"*

Now that's the kind of fiery presence of God I want and need. There is a word in the Bible that describes the power of God. It is the Greek word 'Dunamis'. It speaks of strength, power, and ability. It sounds kind of familiar, doesn't it? That's because it is where we get the English words, 'dynamite, and dynamic'. We all know that dynamite is powerful stuff. A dynamic person is someone who is "positive in attitude and full of energy and new ideas." You get the idea. Dunamis is the power that raised Jesus from the dead. God's miracle-working power is the kind that heals, restores, and resurrects dead things. Without it, our endeavours for The Kingdom are only futile and without substance. We can pray all we like, but if we do it in the flesh rather than by the power of the Holy Spirit to stimulate change, our prayers will be impotent rather than potent. A fire-filled person who operates within God's Dunamis power could be described as a dynamic person. The dictionary defines the noun dynamic as *"a force that stimulates change or progress within a system or process."* Since this book is all about embracing the process, I thought this was quite interesting. Dunamis is just that, a force that stimulates change or progress within the refinement process that God is taking us through to become all that He created us to be. It is this miracle-working force that stimulates change and empowers our progress. We could stumble through the process without it, but it is only when we truly embrace God's power within us that we will step into our destiny and be all that God created us to be.

This same power is what gives us the strength to persevere through the process, and then later, when we transition into the calling that God has for us, this power will achieve what we could never accomplish in our own strength. *"Never doubt God's mighty power to work in you and accomplish all this. He will achieve infinitely more than your greatest request, your most unbelievable dream, and exceed your wildest imagination! He will outdo them all, for his miraculous power constantly energizes you."* Ephesians 3:20 (TPT)

Acts 23:11 (TPT) tells us that Paul received miracle power.

"That night, our Lord appeared to Paul, stood before him, and said, "Receive miracle power. For just as you have spoken for me in Jerusalem, you will also speak for me in Rome." In the NIV, it says, "take courage." Holy Spirit is actually offering supernatural courage that will empower him to complete His mission. God knows that Paul could not do what He asked him to do without this "miracle power". Neither does God expect us to be able to fulfil our destiny without it.

So how do we assure that our words and actions have the potency of God's dunamis power? How do we light the fire or ignite the dynamite as it were? We first must recognise and acknowledge that without God, we are nothing. Secondly, we acknowledge who we are in Christ. It is no longer we that live, but Christ lives in us. He has the power. Therefore we have the power because we are made in His image and have Christ in us. Jesus told His disciples that they would do even greater things than He did while on Earth. We must operate within the Spirit rather than in our own strength. Remember when the disciples first experienced the fire of God? It was in the upper room during the festival of Pentecost. They received the gift of tongues. Being filled to the brim and flooding over with the Holy Spirit and speaking in tongues is a way that we can tap into God's power. When we speak in tongues, we are infused and empowered with God's strength. Romans 8:26a (TPT) *"And in a similar way, the Holy Spirit takes hold of us in our human frailty to empower us in our weakness..."*

I know firsthand what this is like. One day I was attending a special training day at our church. I wasn't feeling at my best. In fact, I was feeling sad, disappointed, and weak. You see, I have always dreamt of recording some of my original songs in a professional studio. When a mentor suggested that my songs were worthy of being recorded, I was highly excited. She put me in touch with a Christian recording studio here in NZ. I emailed them some examples of my songs, and they agreed that I should record them. By now, I was feeling ecstatic! My dreams were about to become a reality. I waited with bated breath for the email with the details of pricing to arrive. When the email finally came, I scanned the page. My face dropped. I felt all hope drain out of me. I just didn't have that kind of money! My dream died that day. Now, don't get me wrong. I'm not saying that dream will never become a reality for me. However, that's how I felt at that moment. And so that weekend, as I walked into the church, I was grieving the loss of a dream. Worse, the training that day was based all around pursuing your dreams. Talk about timing! We were standing in the auditorium receiving a 'pep-talk' from our pastor. He said he was going to have us come forward for ministry .

I thought to myself, "heck, if I go up there, I'm just going to blubber all over the place." I truly felt weak and drained and un-empowered. Next, we were directed to stand in two lines facing toward an assigned partner. I felt a bit panicked, but that is when Holy Spirit prompted me to begin speaking in tongues. While everyone was assembling into two lines, I began to pray in my Spirit language, and do you know what? Within minutes I felt stronger. By the end of the exercise I was prophesying over my partner, and I felt God's power physically surging through my body! That day, I truly came to understand the importance of speaking in tongues. It not only expresses what we can't always articulate to God but it also edifies our spirit and empowers us in a supernatural way.

Prayer, praise, and prophecy are other ways that we can tune into and operate within God's power rather than in our own strength. I will talk more about these in the following chapters.

Chapter 2

Proclamation & Praise

There are more ways than one to proclaim something. Proclamation is not just making a statement with our mouth. How we behave, and even how we present ourselves to the world also makes a statement. We can say something with our mouth and then do something entirely different. Which makes the greater statement? God's creation proclaims who He is. Creation can't speak in words. It proclaims who God is simply by being what God created it to be. The same is true of you and I.

Praise on the other hand is our response to what is being proclaimed. When I look at a beautiful sunset or hear the waves crashing on the beach and see the curve of the waves glimmer with the early morning rays of the rising sun, my heart responds in praise of the one who created this awe-inspiring scene! Praise does not merely come from our lips. It begins in our heart—with our attitude. When we do not appreciate creation, we dishonour The Creator. This includes mankind. We are created in God's image. When we judge others or even judge ourselves, we dishonour Him. But when we appreciate other's and ourselves and what we have to offer the world, we bring praise and honour to God.

CHAPTER 2 - PROCLAMATION & PRAISE

"I prefer living in colour."

— *DAVID HOCKNEY*

Proclaim:

1. To announce or declare in an open or ostentatious way: *to proclaim one's opinions.*
2. To indicate or make known publicly or openly.
3. To extol or praise publicly: *Let them proclaim the Lord.*

Praise:

1. The act of expressing approval or admiration; commendation; laudation.
2. The offering of grateful homage in words or song, as an act of worship: *a hymn of praise to God.*
3. The state of being approved or admired.

Take a good look at the world around you. There is so much beauty, colour, and texture on show—a feast for our senses. God is so creative. His creation is stunning, inspiring, and immensely complex! Psalm 91:1 (NLT) says, *"The heavens proclaim the glory of God. The skies display His craftsmanship."* The word 'proclaim' in a Biblical sense means "to be conspicuous." God's creation —His workmanship, is on display for all to see and to declare God's glory—to point man towards who God is. We are also God's handiwork. Ephesians 2:10 (NLT) says, *"For we are God's masterpiece. (AMP - His workmanship), He has created us anew in Christ Jesus, so we can do the good things He planned for us long ago."* Our purpose is to proclaim who He is; to stand out, be conspicuous, and shine.

So, what exactly does it mean for us to shine, and why is it important? Dictionary.com defines it as follows:

- *To be bright with reflected light; glisten; sparkle.*

Chapter 2 - Proclamation & Praise | 15

- *(of light) to appear brightly or strongly, especially uncomfortably so: Wear dark glasses so the sun won't shine in your eyes.*
- *to be or appear unusually animated or bright, as the eyes or face.*
- *to appear with brightness or clearness, as feelings.*
- **to excel or be conspicuous:** *to shine in school.*

Light doesn't hide. It makes itself known. Does the thought of being conspicuous scare you? Some people are quite happy to be in the limelight. They don't mind being seen, but for those who are shy and introverted, it can be a frightening prospect. However, God created both introverts and extroverts, and He wants them all to shine. Think of it like this. There are different strengths of light. Some are brighter than others, but they are all still lights. They all shine. Your introverted light might be more of a warm glow rather than a blinding spotlight like your flamboyant, extroverted counterpart, and that's ok. JUST DON'T HIDE YOUR LIGHT!

Be the best version of you that you can be—holding nothing back. Excel at being uniquely you! *...We're free of it! All of us! Nothing between us and God, our faces shining with the brightness of his face. And so we are transfigured much like the Messiah, our lives gradually becoming brighter and more beautiful as God enters our lives and we become like him.* 2 Corinthians 3:18 (MSG)

JUST DON'T HIDE YOUR

BE THE BEST VERSION OF
YOU THAT YOU CAN BE.
HOLDING
NOTHING BACK.

We are a reflection of God Himself! That's right. Just as it says in the verse above, we are shining with God's glory. The world needs God's light. We can't afford to hide our light under a bushel, as it says in Matthew 5:14-16 (MSG)

"Here's another way to put it: You're here to be light, bringing out the God-colours in the world. God is not a secret to be kept. We're going public with this, as public as a city on a hill. If I make you light-bearers, you don't think I'm going to hide you under a bucket, do you? I'm putting you on a light stand. Now that I've put you there on a hilltop, on a light stand—shine! Keep open house; be generous with your lives. By opening up to others, you'll prompt people to open up with God, this generous Father in heaven." In surrendering to God's refining process, you are allowing Him to polish you up so that you shine—proclaiming God's glory. That is what the process is all about— being transformed into the

image of God so that in all you say and do, your very being will point people to God. Not only that. Shiny things bring out the shine in other reflective surfaces. You were created to bring out the shine in others. When you shine brightly, you bring out the colour and shine in other people. You have the capability to change the atmosphere around you. When you live your identity in Christ with confidence, the people around you will be inspired to do the same. My ultimate goal would be to reach the point where I am totally comfortable in my own skin, and completely confident in my God-given identity, and I want to encourage you to do the same.

Now let's take a look at a Biblical character who encapsulates this idea. I am inspired by a little story that we read about in 1 Samual chapter 6:14-15 (NLT) *"And David danced before the Lord with all his might, wearing a priestly garment. So David and all the people of Israel brought up the Ark of the Lord with shouts of joy and the blowing of rams' horns."* David is celebrating. He is dancing, and he is doing it publicly! David doesn't care what anyone thinks. He is going all out in complete abandon and extravagant worship before the Lord. I love the picture that it paints in my mind. Have you ever been dancing or singing your little heart out—just going for it, I mean, you're belting out a tune at the top of your lungs feeling happy and carefree, and then, boom; someone walks in on your happy little scene, and you're suddenly very self-conscious and feeling like a complete idiot? Well, that's what David was doing, only I'm pretty sure he knew he wasn't alone, AND HE DIDN'T CARE! That's what I'm talking about. I want to be like that! Sadly I'm not, but that is my goal, and God is working in me towards that end.

Now take a look at verse 16. David's wife was watching and was filled with contempt for him. Then in verses 20 and 21, it says that, *"David retorted to Michal, "I was dancing before the Lord, who chose me above your father and all his family! He appointed me as the leader of Israel, the people of the Lord, so I celebrate before the Lord. Yes, <u>and I am willing to look even more foolish than this, even to be humiliated in my own eyes!</u> But those servant girls you mentioned will indeed think I am distinguished!"* When you shine, not everyone will respond positively! Some people can't stand to see other people succeed. Like David's wife, for example. She looked down her nose at David because she thought it was undignified for a king to behave that way. But, do you know what? I think that's why the people loved David. He had a heart after God. He wasn't so proud that he couldn't humble himself before the Lord in this way. He was a man of the people—he had a good rapport with everyday people just as Christ did. Christ was loved by the people, but he too, was not always popular with everyone! Learning to accept that not everyone loves and supports you is the first step to being confident and comfortable enough in your own skin to be able to live your best life. Even though there will always be a minority of people who don't necessarily like you, the world needs you to be authentically you! People are drawn to authenticity!

When you
SHINE
NOT EVERYONE WILL
RESPOND POSITIVELY

Let me tell a little story to explain why being who you were created to be is so important. A bunch of animals were going through basic training for the 'Animal Army'. The commander gave orders for the animals to climb to the very top of a tall tree. The mouse scuttled his way up the tree trunk as fast as his little legs could carry him, until breathless, he finally made it to the very top. The monkey used his long and dexterous limbs to reach the top of the tree in record time. The eagle didn't actually climb his way up the tree, he found his own more unconventional method. Flapping his wings, he quickly flew into the air and perched on the top branch. The fish, however, had no hope! He completely failed the exercise. The next day they were given another task. This time they were ordered to swim out to the middle of the lake, dive down, and return to the shore underwater. Well, of course, this was an absolute breeze for the fish. The monkey made a really good attempt at it, but made very little headway as he flapped and splashed about. The mouse, poor thing, got halfway out, then ran out of puf and nearly drowned. The eagle picked up the mouse in his talons just in the nick of time and returned him to the safety of dry land. You get the idea, right? Fish were never designed to climb trees! He was set up to fail that task before he even started. In the same way, there are certain things that we as individuals were never designed to do. It's not much wonder that we feel like a failure when we try to be someone we were never designed to be. Comparison kills uniqueness, confidence, and authenticity. *"Make a careful exploration of who you are and the work you have been given, and then sink yourself into that. Don't be impressed with yourself. Don't compare yourself with others. Each of you must take responsibility for doing the creative best you can with your own life."* Galatians 6:4-5 (MSG). We are His masterpiece, created in Christ Jesus to do good works that He prepared in advance for us to do." (Eph 2:10). A masterpiece is a one-off work of art. There is no other like it. You and I are a one-off work of art! It is silly to try to be a copy when the original is so much more valuable.

What if God withheld His creativity from us because we don't always appreciate it or respond to it the way we should? It just doesn't bare thinking about. Imagine a world without colour. A whole element of beauty and variety would be missing. Without colour the world could be a very dreary place. Why is it then that so many women opt for a colourless wardrobe? I used to wear a lot of black, until I discovered that certain colours suit me. When I wear the colours that suit me, I look good and feel good. I have nothing against black. It serves its purpose. However, I prefer to embrace a world of colour; in fact, I absolutely love colour. Did you know that there is just about a colour for every mood? The colour black often represents depression and grief. Yes, that's why people have been wearing it to funerals for 100's of years. So, I ask again, why has black become such a staple in our wardrobes? Maybe because we have all bought into the lie that black makes us look thinner. This is not necessarily true. I guess it helps us to blend in. It feels safe, right? But who wants to be restricted to a boring, 'safe' life? Well, that's my opinion anyway. Don't get me wrong. Black definitely has it's place. It's a great staple in your wardrobe, and I know some women who do genuinely look good in black, but even those women should feel confident to wear other colours that suit them as well!

Personally, I'd rather live a life of colour, and I'm inviting you to do the same. Colour makes me feel cheerful. Colour makes me feel confident. Yes, colour can even make me feel secure! When I wear the colours that suit me, I feel good. When I feel good, I'm confident, cheerful, and secure. The right colour accentuates our eyes. Now, when I say colour, that doesn't just mean bright, way out colours. It can mean that, but colour can also be soft and subtle. Some people suit soft and subtle; others don't. Don't be afraid to explore colour. Find what suits you.

Colour can have the opposite effect too—if you wear the wrong ones. We are all unique. Our skin colour, eye colour, and hair colour, among other things, have an impact on what colours we look good in. The more you look into this concept, the more you discover that the colours you wear reflect aspects of your personality. Colours have tints, tones, and shades. This happens when you add either black, white, or grey to a colour in its true state. If you add white, you get tints. Add Black and you get shades of colour, and adding grey gives you tones. White always adds a sense of lightness and brightness. Grey softens colours, and black gives depth. Now consider these elements. Light and bright. Does this bring a person to mind? What about soft and gentle? Now think about the word 'depth.' This would be someone who has substance—they have a solid, dependable nature, and perhaps more of a serious side. Get the idea? I am not an expert on this topic. However, I have always had an interest in personality profiling. I love exploring the idea that we are all different, and yet we seem to fit into certain patterns or categories of personality types, and this seems to be the case with colour as well. Have you ever noticed someone wearing a particular colour, and you thought to yourself, "they look good in that?" I am artistic and creative, and I have always had an eye for colour. I just seem to have an instinct. I often say to people, "that colour really suits you." Even so, I have sought out information about what to wear from some of the experts over the years. Remember Trinny and Susannah? I also had my colours assessed a couple of times by a colour specialist. There seem to be a few different methods and opinions about the right way of doing it so it can be a little confusing. Don't let that put you off. Take it all with a grain of salt. Glean what you can, but also go with your instincts. Experiment, and don't be afraid to get it wrong sometimes! At least you tried. Better to try and be a little bit off than to stick to wearing black by default and not even try. Don't you want to look and feel at your best? I recently discovered Carol Tuttle - "Dressing Your Truth". I don't necessarily advocate everything she teaches; however, I have found her free beginner's guide to "Dressing Your Truth" very helpful! She talks not only about colour, but also pattern, design, shape, and even facial features to determine what you should wear. Wear colour, and wear it with confidence. Discover what colours, shapes, styles, and patterns enhance your natural personality. So why am I going on about wearing colour? Isn't God more concerned with what is on the inside rather than our outward appearance? Absolutely! But who we are; what we do, what we say, and how we portray ourselves to the world, is ALL a reflection of our God. God is so creative - so beautiful - so colourful. Why shouldn't we express ourselves in the same way?

Don't be afraid to stand out. I say that with a warning! There's standing out in the crowd for a good reason and then there is standing out like a sore thumb! My journey with colour began at an early age. My dad has always been quite a flashy dresser. He likes to stand out. I'm probably like my father, but I have had a few bad experiences that knocked my confidence and caused me a lifelong battle with my self- image. The things that happen in our early years tend to do that. They shape us, for better or worse, and unless we concentrate some effort in dealing with these issues, they can hold us in bondage for the rest of our lives. In 1984 we had just returned from the mission field permanently. We didn't own much more than the clothes on our back, and those clothes were not designed for the New Zealand climate. So it was off to see Mrs. Hewlett. Mrs. Hewlett had a garage full of second-hand clothing, and so she allowed the poor missionary family to come and pick out a new wardrobe. I was ten years old. I remember one particular outfit that just gives me the horror when I think of it. I don't know if it was me who picked out the canary yellow, towelling tracksuit or perhaps my mother? Now looking back, I absolutely cringe! How did anyone ever think that would be a fashion statement? But I said I liked colour, right? Yeah, well, that tracksuit made a statement but not the kind I wanted to make. I mean, sure, there must be a few characters out there that could pull off such a loud and proud outfit, but that person is not me. Thank goodness I was only ten and didn't know any better, but there have been many times since then where I have worn an outfit and felt, either over-dressed or under-dressed for the occasion, and whenever that happened, I felt ashamed. Why? Why should what we wear determine our value? This brings to mind two well-known sayings. "You are what you wear," and " clothes make the man." What does this mean, and is it really true?

Studies have shown that what we wear really does have an impact on how people perceive us, and even how we feel about ourselves. People who dress more conservatively are seen as being more reliable and trustworthy. A woman who wears a more masculine outfit like a suit to an interview is often more likely to be hired. One study even showed that when someone wore a white lab coat understood to belong to a doctor, they were more focused and performed better than if they were wearing a white coat that they were told belonged to a painter. Over the ages, clothes have been a means of signifying a person's social or economic status, culture, moral standards, religious beliefs, and enforcing differences in class. In Japan, the colour and weave of a kimono, the way it's worn, and the size and stiffness of the sash demonstrate the person's social rank. In China, yellow robes were used exclusively for the emperor. The Houysa tribe of Africa, who were members of the ruling aristocracy, wore huge turbans on their heads and several layers of expensive clothing in imported cloth which increased their body size, setting them apart from the rest of their society.

Fortunately, in the western world today, there is not so much of a distinction between classes, but even so, sadly, I see many people who put themselves into debt in order to look a certain way—in order to be perceived as wealthy or popular or whatever. I am not endorsing this at all! Clothes should not have power over us. It should never determine our value. We should not be dictated to by the latest trends. Things like beauty and fashion, and style are so subjective. Look at any of the sculptures and paintings from the Renaissance era, for example. The women were all let's just say, 'very well rounded.' They are the product of the culture and values that were predominant at the time. This is very different from the standards of beauty these days. What supposedly looks stylish now, quite possibly when we look back in ten- or twenty-years' time, will be perceived as ugly or downright laughable. So, all this said, don't put too much time, energy, or money into what you wear, but do have fun with it. We can learn to appropriately utilize clothing to look and feel our best; wearing clothes that express the authentic personality and beauty that lies within us. If you're a curvy woman, embrace those curves. Make the most of them. If you are less curvy and more straight up and down, there are so many styles that you can wear to give you a lovely feminine shape. Whatever colour, size, or shape you are, learn to love it. God made you that way.

At the beginning of this year, I participated in a five-day challenge to prophetically plan out the year. Every day we were given an activation activity to complete towards this plan. On day one, we were asked to seek God for a 'word' for the year. Generally, this would be one word—something to act as a kind of theme for the year. For example, it might be something like; 'Collaboration', 'breakthrough', or 'authority'. The 'word'. I received was actually more than one word. It was; 'relax and enjoy." On day two, we were asked to write ourselves a letter from God further elaborating on this word. This is what the Lord spoke to me. *"Dear Lisa, I am crazy about you. Don't care too much about what anyone else thinks. I made you, and I say you are awesome! Rest in that. Relax in your identity and enjoy who you are, even if not everyone else does. When you enjoy you –I enjoy you. When you relax and enjoy yourself, you become such a blessing to others. Yes, you will annoy some, but that is because they are not resting in their own identity. You have to let that go! Don't focus on the one or two that you might offend – focus on the many you will bless."* I want that! I want to be able to feel relaxed about who I am. I want to enjoy my identity—what makes me, me. I want to be unafraid to be who I was created to be, but I am my own worst enemy. What about you—are you comfortable in your own skin, or like me, do you tell yourself you're not good enough, beautiful enough, clever enough, or simply not enough? It is an ongoing battle for me. You know—that voice in your head that sends you conflicting messages all the time. Here I am writing a whole book about how we should shine, and yet I still grapple with this issue myself. Sometimes I just want to withdraw—to run and hide. When you shine, it won't always be appreciated. People may be jealous of your success or feel intimidated by you when you embrace who you really are. There seems to be some innate desire to put others down to make us feel better about ourselves. We feel lesser-than when we compare ourselves to others, and so instead of celebrating their triumphs, we tear them down to size, or at the very least, we don't give them any praise or encouragement. The truth is, they are not your competition. They are running in a completely different race than you. You can both be winners in your own race, and you don't need to compare. Just because they win their race doesn't mean you've lost yours! Their success or failure is no reflection of you. Run your race and run it with excellence. Celebrate each other's wins, and console and encourage one another when you lose. It's ok for you both to shine!

Learn to love yourself—that's the key. When we compare ourselves to others, we will never measure up. We are not meant to. Why? Because we are all different. I was not created to look the same as you. Neither was I created to act the same way as you, or fulfil the same destiny. You do it your way, and I'll do it mine. That's how it should be. We are accountable to God. He is the one who created us. He is the one with the plan for our lives—things that He prepared in advance for us to do (Eph 2:10). When God was creating everything, as He finished each one, He described them as good! The word 'good' in Hebrew means beautiful, pleasant, and agreeable. Psalm 139:14 tells us that God's works are marvellous—we are fearfully and wonderfully made. In Hebrew, to be wonderfully made means, "to be separated or distinct—set apart," and marvellously means "to be surpassing or extraordinary." This is describing you. What God did in creating you can only be described as extraordinary! You are distinct—set apart! This means you should be different—unique. As it says in Romans 12:2 (TPT) *"Stop imitating the ideals and opinions of the culture around you, but be inwardly transformed by the Holy Spirit through a total reformation of how you think. This will empower you to discern God's will as you live a beautiful life, satisfying and perfect in his eyes."* If you want to look and feel beautiful, don't measure yourself by the ideals and opinions of the culture around you. Let God's standard be your benchmark. It will take a change in thinking. You will have to challenge your self-talk and the thoughts that assail you. It's going to take some effort! The prevalent messages that besiege us through advertising and social media assert that we are not good enough! That is what the enemy wants us to believe. We have to make an active decision not to give in to this pattern of thinking. Whose opinion matters to you the most? Is it the fear of God or the fear of man that motivates you? I am totally preaching to myself here. I struggle in this area as much as the next person. It is an ongoing battle for me, but as long as I can look back and see that there has been growth and transformation in my life then, great! I'm on the right track. It's all a process, right? So long as you and I are headed in the right direction, we can celebrate our triumphs and give ourselves a break when we don't always get it right.

Now one last story to illustrate this point. A couple of nights ago, I had a dream. It wasn't anything special really, but it was funny. I actually woke myself up laughing. In the morning, I thought to myself. What was that all about? Why did I dream that? Then it hit me. God gave me this dream to add to this book as a funny little reminder to us to be authentic. In the dream, a woman was swimming in a pool. She says to a man, "Give this swimsuit to her. Women like to look sexy." The her that she was referring to can only be described as Dawn French from the TV program "The Vicor Of Dibley." If you don't know who I mean, look her up on YouTube. She is rather voluptuous or busty if you know what I mean? Well, the next thing I see 'Dawn' comes out proudly parading in her new swimsuit. It was a very comedic sight. The swimsuit did fit her for the most part, but there was one problem. The swimsuit had padded cups in the top like a padded bra; only the cups were a circular shape and about four sizes too small! It really tickled my fancy, and as I said, I woke up laughing my head off and nearly woke my husband up! The message that God wanted me to get across through this little example was this: Do not try to fit into a mould you were never designed to fit into! that's like an 'F'cup trying to fit into an 'A' cup as in the illustration above. The PROCESS of refinement is all about learning to live in your true identity as bearers of God's image. Learning to embrace the process brings transformation—from glory to glory. 2 Corinthians 3:18 (TPT)... *"We are being transfigured into his very image as we move from one brighter level of glory to another."* We were created to shine; to shine like a beautiful diamond. Embrace the process. Allow God, the master jeweller to polish you to bring out the beauty and potential in you.

You might wonder why I have spent so much time talking about our outward appearance in this chapter. Apart from the fact that it is a subject that I enjoy, I also believe that what we portray to the outside world is just an overflow of who we are on the inside. Every part of our identity is a proclamation of who our creator is. Well, it should be anyway. When we are living in the spirit and exhibiting who God intended us to be, that is. The Bible says that what's on the inside will be evident on the outside. You can't hide it. Therefore, it is even more important how we are on the inside. How can we accurately proclaim who God is without having an intimate relationship with Him? By spending time filling ourselves up with the word of God and letting the spirit of God 'rub off on us. The more time we spend with Him, the more we become like Him, and that can't help but show on the outside. We want it to show on the outside, right? Then we have to allow ourselves to be conspicuous. We need to shine!

The Bible says in Matthew 12:34-35 (TPT) *"But you who are known as the Pharisees are rotten to the core like venomous snakes. How can your words be good if you are rotten within? For what has been stored up in your hearts will be heard in the overflow of your words! "When virtue is stored within, the hearts of good, upright people will produce good fruit. But when evil is hidden within, those who are evil will produce evil fruit."* Let's delve into this scripture a bit. The most obvious example of the word proclaim is our speech, but a less obvious example is the way we act. The latter part of the verse tells us that what is in our hearts will be exposed through our actions. Remember our definition of the word proclaim? One of those definitions was "to indicate or make known publicly or openly." Our actions 'proclaim' the state of our hearts.

So what has all this got to do with the topic of this book — "embracing the process"? I'm glad you asked. The process that we go through during the 'in-between' transforms us on the inside. As difficult as this time can be, it is an opportunity for us to draw near to the Father. During these times, it may feel like nothing is happening, but I assure you it is. In my example, I was 'just' a stay-at-home mum who homeschooled her children. I was desperate to get out and do something important. I have to laugh. I knew that this role was important, but my attitude didn't really reflect that. I undervalued it. Life felt very mundane. I wanted to be off on mission trips or some other ministry activity. Over the past 21 years of raising my children—nurturing and shaping their character, God was doing the same with me! Recently I completed a 21-day process of reconceptualising a toxic thought that I have allowed to take root in my life. Dr Caroline Leaf, a Christian neuroscientist, has an app that takes you through a step-by-step process of reconceptualisation and healing. My toxic thought? That, "nothing ever changes, nothing exciting happens in my life, and I have no control". On day twenty-one, we were asked to write down a newly formed statement which we are then to speak out loud once a day for another 43 days—the time it takes for our brains to physically construct and confirm a new thought. Every day I make this statement out loud, "Who I am now is more beautiful and amazing than if I'd had a perfect, easy life. Delay is not denial. Delay is ok. God does bring about good and exciting changes in my life. I am growing and maturing in Him as I wait patiently and trust Him to be in control." Learning to trust God is the first step to embracing the process of becoming all that God created us to be.

I have a confession to make. With all this talk of proclamation—a topic I am obviously passionate about, I completely forgot to mention anything about praise, and here I am, a worship leader! It only just dawned on me now after reading through the document I received back from my editor. Praise is such an important topic that it cannot be omitted.

Praise is a crucial part of our growth and transformation. It is a choice we make. When we are in the midst of the process; feeling impatient for change, and impatient for God to move—when things may not be going the way we would like them to we may not feel like praising, but that is exactly what we need to do. Sometimes we have to fake it till we make it. It is an act of obedience. Our hearts may not be fully invested in the beginning, but as we continue to surrender our hearts in praise and worship, there will be a shift. Praise diverts our thoughts and emotions into alignment with God's truth. Praise reminds us who God is, what He has done for us, and what He is capable of doing for us in the future. It awakens faith and hope. When we choose to praise even when we would rather just curl up in a ball and cry or feel sorry for ourselves, our circumstances may not change, but our attitude will, and so will the whole atmosphere around us. Satan hates praise unless it is directed at him, that is. I like to think of praise as a kind of force field that surrounds us and makes the enemy flee. Praise God in the good times and the bad. Praise has the power to lift you up when you are down. Praise places God in His rightful place, seated on the throne above any of your troubles or circumstances. Praise has the power to overcome depression or despondency. Praise moves us toward God and towards our destiny. Lastly, praise is not just singing to God. It is a heart attitude that can also be expressed in what we say and do. Praise is a heart of gratitude rather than a mouth full of complaints. 1 Thessalonians 5:16-18 (MSG) "Be cheerful no matter what; pray all the time; thank God no matter what happens. This is the way God wants you who belong to Christ Jesus to live." Praise is also a sacrifice. Hebrews 13:15-16 (TPT) "So we no longer offer up a steady stream of blood sacrifices, but through Jesus, we will offer up to God a steady stream of praise sacrifices—these are "the lambs" we offer from our lips that celebrate his name! We will show mercy to the poor and not miss an opportunity to do acts of kindness for others, for these are the true sacrifices that delight God's heart."

And so, we recognise that praise is a very important part of the 'polishing' process. Praise may not change our current circumstances, but it will change us, and that is what the process is all about. My Grandmother once said to my mother, "you want your children to be happy, don't you?" My mother replied, "of course I want my children to be happy, but there is something much more important that I want for them, and that is that they are all that God created them to be—holy and consecrated to Him. The same is true of our Heavenly Father. While He is concerned with our happiness, He is more concerned with our Holiness. The journey to becoming and accomplishing all God has planned for us will not be an easy one, but ultimately stepping into our destiny will produce joy in us that will cause us to shine and will overflow into the world around us, bringing others into relationship with God and ultimately into their own destinies.

Chapter 3

Pressure & Pain

PAIN! It's not a nice subject and one I would rather avoid, but pain is a necessary part of life. There is a very rare congenital condition where people are born without sensitivity to physical pain. This inability to feel often leads to an accumulation of bruises, broken bones, wounds, and other health issues. Pain is our bodies way of protecting us from harm. It's a warning that our bodies are in danger or that something is wrong.

There are also mental health issues that cause people to feel numb emotionally. This insensitivity to emotions is also an indication that something is wrong. I would rather not feel negative emotions but I understand that to live a healthy life emotionally, we need to allow ourselves to feel. Avoiding or suppressing emotional pain only delays the inevitable. It will come out somehow, some way and probably not in a healthy way. It may even cause physical issues if we don't deal with it. That doesn't mean that we should wallow in our pain and never move on. The first step is to acknowledge our pain—to identify it and tell God all about it. You may also need someone you can trust to help you process those feelings. A trusted pastor or counsellor. If it is too painful to go there, take it in short doses. Dr Caroline Leaf has some amazing resources to help in this area. Check her out on Google or YouTube. She has an app that I found very helpful called "Neurocycle".
Here's the link: https://apps.apple.com/us/app/neurocycle/id1460119837

Are you experiencing any pain? What might this physical or emotional pain be trying to warn you about? Sometimes physical pain is a response to emotional pain or pressure (stress). Dealing with the emotional pain can help to alleviate the physical pain. Are you ready to take steps toward dealing with this pain? Who could you ask for help?

CHAPTER 3 - PRESSURE AND PAIN

"Pressure can burst a pipe, or pressure can make a diamond."

— ROBERT HORRY

Pressure:
The state of being pressed or compressed - a constraining or compelling force or influence - urgency, or exertion of force.
Pain:

1. Physical suffering or distress, as due to injury, illness, etc.
2. A distressing sensation in a particular part of the body: a back pain.
3. Mental or emotional suffering or torment: I am sorry my news causes you such pain.

You and I both know pressure can be an ugly word! We all experience it pretty much on a daily basis. It sometimes helps us to stay motivated, but can also leave us feeling stressed and exhausted. There is pressure all around us. Pressure to perform a certain way, pressure to look good, and pressure to be healthy, beautiful, thin, intelligent, successful; the pressure to be the good Christian—the amazing multi-tasking mum with a successful career AND amazingly talented children too. The list could go on and on. But, let me ask you this; where is this pressure coming from? I understand that a lot of the pressure is coming from an external source—the media, Facebook, Instagram, advertising, even from the pulpit, but what is important is how we respond to these pressures. You must admit, we are often our own worst enemies. We put pressure on ourselves. This sort of pressure does not come from God. I venture to say that although God IS interested in our personal growth and transformation, He DOES NOT put these kinds of demands on us. He orchestrates the circumstances of our lives to shape us into His image—working with us as we cooperate with the Holy Spirit in our lives. He pinpoints areas in our lives that need addressing, and this can feel uncomfortable.

In our Christian walk, pressure is a necessary part of growth and development. In Romans 5:3-4 (TPT), we see an example of this, *"But that's not all! Even in times of trouble, we have a joyful confidence, knowing that our pressures will develop in us patient endurance. And patient endurance will refine our character, and proven character leads us back to hope."* Pressure is one of the important components in the process of creating a diamond, and if you want to shine like the diamond you are, then inevitably, you will experience some pressure. The word pressure used here in the Passion translation is the Greek word Thlipsis which is translated as "tribulation." **Usage:** persecution, affliction, distress, tribulation.

HELPS Word-studies 2347 thlípsis – properly, pressure (what constricts or rubs together), used of a narrow place that "hems someone in"; tribulation, especially internal pressure that causes someone to feel confined (restricted, "without options").

2347/thlípsis ("compression, tribulation") carries the challenge of coping with the internal pressure of a tribulation, especially when feeling there is "no way of escape" ("hemmed in"). Now let's take a look at some other verses that use this word. In John 16:33, Jesus tells us that in this world we will have tribulation. This is translated as 'trouble' in some Bible translations. So what should our response to this kind of pressure be? Romans 12:12 (AMP) says, *"constantly rejoicing in hope [because of our confidence in Christ], steadfast and patient in distress, devoted to prayer [continually seeking wisdom, guidance, and strength],"* -A footnote in the Passion Translation tells us to bear our afflictions bravely and with joy. So we can conclude that our response to pressure should be one of joy, patience, and prayer. JOY! Are you kidding me? How on earth do we do that? Real joy goes far deeper than just happiness. Happiness is superficial and can be short lived but joy is more enduring. It abides in our Spirit. It is that confident assurance in God, trusting that He is faithful. He is full of love and wants only the best for us. He will bring good out of our tribulation. How does God bring something good out of it? Remember He *"causes everything to work together for the good of those who love God and are called according to his purpose for them."* Romans 8:28 (NLT)

First and foremost, God knows that tribulation develops our spiritual muscles. Just like when we work out at the gym. My gym instructor has just put me on a new routine. I have two circuits. Within each circuit are several different exercises that challenge not only my strength but also my fitness. I have to complete each exercise one after the other without a break, and each circuit three times in a row. The first week, I could barely do some exercises, but now I'm three weeks in, my strength and fitness have increased, and those exercises have become a little easier. I must admit though, just between you and me, there are times I do have to take a quick breather to let my heart rate slow down a little. It's really hard work, but I am reaping the benefits. After a hard workout, my body feels great—all those endorphins flooding my bloodstream! I have a number of different physical issues for which I am contending for, so in the meantime, I am doing what I can to assist my body to feel less stiff and sore. Going to the gym is one way I can do that.

Developing strong spiritual muscles works in the same way. Without resistance (just another word for pressure or tribulation), we would not develop any strength of character or maturity. We would be like spiritual babies. *"Brothers and sisters, when I was with you I found it impossible to speak to you as those who are spiritually mature people, for you are still dominated by the mind-set of the flesh. And because you are immature infants in Christ,"* 1 Corinthians 3:1 (TPT)

1 Timothy 4:8-10 (NLT) tells us that *"Physical training is good, but training for godliness is much better, promising benefits in this life and in the life to come." This is a trustworthy saying, and everyone should accept it. This is why we work hard and continue to struggle, for our hope is in the living God, who is the Saviour of all people and particularly of all believers."* I'm afraid to say that pain and pressure are necessary for becoming more mature in Christ. If our desire is to grow, then we will have to embrace the process. Matthew 13:20-21 (TPT) says, *"The one sown on gravel represents the person who gladly hears the kingdom message, but his experience remains shallow. Shortly after he hears it, troubles and persecutions come because of the kingdom message he received. Then he quickly falls away, for the truth didn't sink deeply into his heart."*

Pressure tests our mettle. It tests to see whether we have the courage to carry on. Do we have the heart to follow through when the going gets tough? Do we have the spiritual maturity to endure the pressure?

It may be physical or emotional pain, and it comes in all sorts of shapes and sizes. What one person faces will vary enormously from another. 1 Corinthians 10:13 tells us that EVERYONE will face challenges. It will never seem completely fair, but fortunately, we CAN TRUST GOD to know how much we can handle. I particularly like the Passion Translation, which puts it this way. *"We all experience times of testing, which is normal for every human being. But God will be faithful to you. He will screen and filter the severity, nature, and timing of every test or trial you face so that you can bear it. And each test is an opportunity to trust him more, for along with every trial, God has provided for you a way of escape that will bring you out of it victoriously."* 1 Corinthians 10:13 (TPT)

I have not had a completely easy life, but compared to some of the things many of my good friends have been through, I feel like I have gotten off lightly. It has been difficult to observe one of my closest friends go through hell the last few years. Not just one heart-breaking circumstance, but one after another. The God I serve promises that He has a plan and purpose for our lives. A plan for good and not a disaster. (Jer 29:11) It is disconcerting and confusing when we believe one thing and experience quite another! I know I said that we can trust

Chapter 3 - Pressure And Pain

God, but I get why it might be difficult to trust Him with our future when the past or present has been, or is, such a nightmare! It is easy to say God is good when life is going well, but what about when it all goes to custard? Psalm 27:13 (NLT) says, *"Yet I am confident I will see the Lord's goodness while I am here in the land of the living."* Can you say that with confidence? During those difficult years, my friend was not feeling quite so confident about this, and I don't blame her! I too, began to question my theology. I have grown up with an expectation that God will look after me and my family; protect me, and preserve me. I expect good things to happen. Am I naive in this belief? The Bible is full of positive promises. After some prayer and contemplation, the conclusion I have come to is that we should expect the best but be prepared for the worst. We live in a fallen world. Bad things happen. God never promised that they wouldn't happen to us; in fact, He warns us in John 16:33 (NLT) that, *"Here on earth you will have many trials and sorrows. But take heart, because I have overcome the world."*

I was listening to a podcast earlier this week while I was working out at the gym. This means that I cannot take notes, so the information doesn't always stick in my brain, but there was one particular part that caught my attention. The speaker had just been diagnosed with cancer and was crying out to God, I imagine a bit like Jesus in the Garden of Gethsemane when He asked God to take 'the cup' from Him, meaning find another way to bring about the salvation of mankind so that He didn't have to go through with His crucifixion. She heard God say to her, "I will take you to the basement and sit with you in the dark until fear no longer has a hold on you." In other words, God was not going to remove the dark, painful situation she found herself in. However, He would indeed be with her through it, and not only that; He would bring her to the point of a new maturity in Him to where she was no longer afraid. She was about to walk through the valley of the shadow of death, but she would come to a place where she could honestly say she feared no evil. (Psalm 23:4)

HOPE, dear friends! That is the answer. Hope is a confident expectation of a good and faithful God who has the power to turn it all around. (Romans 8:28)

"GOD proves to be good to the man who passionately waits, to the woman who diligently seeks. It's a good thing to quietly hope, quietly hope for help from GOD. It's a good thing when you're young to stick it out through the hard times.

When life is heavy and hard to take, go off by yourself. Enter the silence. Bow in prayer. Don't ask questions: Wait for hope to appear. Don't run from trouble. Take it full-face. The "worst" is never the worst. Why? Because the Master won't ever walk out and fail to return. If He works severely, He also works tenderly. His stockpiles of loyal love are immense. He takes no pleasure in making life hard, in throwing roadblocks in the way:" Lamentations 3:25-33 (MSG)

Just as God did not remove the difficult circumstances for the women in the podcast I listened to, neither did He stop Jesus from being crucified. I love Hebrews chapter 12. We can learn a lot about processing through pressure and pain from this passage. Let's take a thorough look at verses 1-7 and pick out a few important points.

Point 1: (Heb 12:1a) *"As for us, we have all of these great witnesses who encircle us like clouds.* When you are facing pressure or pain of some kind, remember that there is a "cloud of witnesses", saints who have already passed on to their eternal reward, who have lived through times of difficulty, who understand what we are going through and are now cheering us on, urging us not to give up. We are not on our own, and neither are we the only ones to ever experience pain. 1 Peter 5:9b (TPT) says, *"...For you *know that your believing brothers and sisters around the world are experiencing the same kinds of troubles you endure."*

Point 2: (Heb 12:1b) *"So we must let go of every wound that has pierced us and the sin we so easily fall into.* Going through painful experiences will inadvertently cause all sorts of trauma to our souls. Left unchecked, trauma can lead to sin. This sin may be committed by you, or against you. Either way, sin is involved and needs to be addressed. So how do we do that? Katie Souza teaches that in order to be healed from the wounds in our soul that have come as a result of sin, we need to repent of our part and ask God to cover the sin with His cleansing blood - but don't stop there. We then ask God to allow his resurrection power to flow through us to heal our soul wounds. (For more information on this, check out Katie Souza Ministries.)

Point 3: (Heb 12: 1c) *Then we will be able to run life's marathon race with passion and determination, for the path has been already marked out before us.* A Marathon is painful. It takes endurance. During the often long and painful transformation process, God wants us to know that we can not only endure it but also live with passion and determination because He has a plan. He has already prepared the way. Many other verses talk about this fact in the Bible. Ephesians 2:10 tells us that God prepared good works for us in advance, (or beforehand). Proverbs 3:5 & 6 affirms that if we trust God and acknowledge Him, He will show us which path to take, or as it says in the

Amplified translation, "He will make your paths straight and smooth (removing obstacles that block your way)". You might think that this is a contradiction. On the one hand, I am saying that God allows us to endure pain and hardship for His good purpose, but then this verse is saying that God smooths out the path and removes the obstacles. I'm asking myself the same question. Which is it then? The translation that I learned growing up was that if we trust in the Lord with all our hearts and lean not on our own understanding, He will direct our paths. This seems to make more sense to me. It's not that it's all going to be easy going, but rather God shows us which path to take and then guides us along the way. The path gets steep and a bit treacherous at times, but then psalm 91 says... *"He ordered his angels to guard you wherever you go. If you stumble, they'll catch you; their job is to keep you from falling. You'll walk unharmed among lions and snakes, and kick young lions and serpents from the path."* He walks along with us. Psalm 23:1-4 in the Message translation describes this beautifully. *"God, my shepherd! I don't need a thing. You have bedded me down in lush meadows, you find me quiet pools to drink from. True to your word, you let me catch my breath and send me in the right direction. Even when the way goes through Death Valley, I'm not afraid when you walk at my side."*

Point 4: (Heb 12:2a) *"We look away from the natural realm and we focus our attention and expectation onto Jesus who birthed faith within us and who leads us forward into faith's* *perfection.* Take your focus off earthly circumstances. Ask God to give you a Heavenly perspective. I have found this really helpful in my own experience. For the last 6 and a half years, I have suffered from consistent physical pain. In the beginning, I found it very distressing. Most days, by 5 o'clock in the afternoon, I would be in tears and feeling sore, tired, and distressed. I was very much focused on the physical discomfort I was experiencing, and in truth, that made it all the worse! One day I was journaling, and I said to God, "Is this it for me for the rest of my life. Will I be in pain until the day I die?" Before I had even finished writing out the question, a verse quickly sprung to mind. It was one that God had identified to me in a previous painful season of my life. In fact, I had only recently come through that season and now was faced with another. The previous season was a time of emotional pain. It was pain at a soul level. My heart ached rather than my physical body, but the lesson was the same. I had learned to let go and to trust God in that season, and I needed to do the same in this one.

The verse that God brought to mind was 1 Peter 5:10, which says that after you have suffered a little while, He (God) will restore, strengthen and support you..." I immediately felt that His answer was that it might not happen right away, but He would fully restore me to health. Since then, not only has the pain NOT gone away, but I have developed two other strange and uncomfortable conditions that no one seems to be able to offer any remedy for.

Much like in the previous season of my life, I struggled and strained, cried and complained, and did everything I could think to do, all to no avail, until finally, I surrendered. I concluded that God has promised to heal me, and I just have to trust and surrender to His sovereign timing. Letting go has honestly made my pain lessen, and the fear that comes with it! FEAR is one of the enemy's most potent weapons. I cannot tell you how many times the enemy has reminded me of my mother's words saying, "oh, you're just like your father." My father who is in chronic, excruciating pain that the doctors offer him no cure for, nor much of any kind of relief. Yes, the enemy tries to evoke fear in us by removing all hope. Whenever I feel pain and distress rising up I move my focus from the pain to the promise. Faith, not fear has become my moto. Now let's return to our scripture passage.

Point 5: (Heb 12:2b) *His example is this: Because His heart was focused on the joy of knowing that you would be His, He endured the agony of the cross and conquered its humiliation, and now sits exalted at the right hand of the throne of God!* Follow Christ's example in that He set his eyes on "the joy set before Him". His goal was set. His focus was unwavering. What He set out to accomplish, no matter how difficult, was more important. It was worth the agony. It gave Him great joy to know that His sacrifice meant the joy of bringing us into a relationship with God the Father. What joy can you focus on? Is it the knowledge that God is using this pain or pressure in your life to perfect you, draw you nearer to Him, or impact the lives of those around you?

Point 6: (Heb 12:3) *So consider carefully how Jesus faced such intense opposition from sinners who opposed their own souls, so that you won't become worn down and cave in under life's pressures.* Don't give up! Jesus set the example for us. He faced great opposition to his ministry here on earth, but He never gave up. Everything that you are going through is preparing you for the great things that God has in store for you. So don't give up.

Point 7: (Heb 12:5-7) *"And have you forgotten his encouraging words spoken to you as his children? He said, "My child, don't underestimate the value of the discipline and training of the Lord God, or get depressed when He has to correct you. For the Lord's training of your life is the evidence of his faithful love. And when He draws you to himself, it proves you are his delightful child." Fully embrace God's correction as part of your training, for He is doing what any loving father does for his children. For who has ever heard of a child who never had to be corrected?"* Pressure, described here as discipline or training, is something to be embraced, as difficult as that is. Like a loving parent, we know that God disciplines us to help us mature and is a sign of His love and care for us.

We all know the story of Joseph and the coat of many colours, right? Well, at least if you went to Sunday School, then you surely would have heard it. If you haven't read it lately, you can find it in Genesis chapters 37

- 50. Joseph's story stands out to me as an example of how God uses our suffering and hardship for good. But did Joseph understand that his suffering was not in vain? At the time, probably not. When we are going through difficult circumstances, we aren't focused so much on the outcome. We just want out! God used suffering not only to develop Joseph's character but also for the benefit of others for generations to come. (Genesis 46:6-27) With everything that Joseph was going through, he couldn't have known; couldn't have predicted the good that would come of it. Joseph didn't know that the whole Israelite nation's survival depended on his response to difficult circumstances. Joseph was given authority in the very sphere of his biggest failures and hardship. What about you? Can you look back and see how you have grown? Have the difficulties you've been through led you to the point where you now have the authority to speak into other people's situations to help them through the process from promise to fulfilment of their destiny? How will you respond to the pressure that you are under now? Will you fight it, or will you surrender to the process?

God doesn't rescue us from every difficulty. I read this on Facebook recently, and It sums up this chapter beautifully. God could rescue us, but He knows the whole story from beginning to end. I know it seems hard, but embrace the process. God is doing mighty work in and through you. We can trust that He knows best.

"I WOULD HAVE PULLED JOSEPH out. Out of that pit. Out of that prison. Out of that pain. I would have cheated nations out of the one God would use to deliver them from famine.

I WOULD HAVE pulled David out. Out of Saul's spear-throwing presence. Out of the caves, he hid away from the pain of rejection. I would have cheated Israel out of a Godhearted king.

I WOULD HAVE pulled Esther out. Out of being snatched from her only family. Out of being placed in a position she never asked for. Out of the path of a vicious, power-hungry foe. I would have cheated a people out of the woman God would use to save their very lives.

I WOULD HAVE pulled Jesus off. Off of the cross. Off of the road that led to suffering and pain. Off of the path, that would mean nakedness and beatings, nails and thorns. I would have cheated the entire world out of a Saviour. Out of salvation. Out of an eternity filled with no more suffering and no more pain.

AND OH FRIEND, I want to pull you out. I want to change your path. I want to stop your pain. But right now, I know I would be wrong. I would be out of line. I would be cheating you and cheating the world out of so much good because God knows. He knows the good this pain will produce. He knows the beauty of this hardship will grow. He's watching over you and keeping you even in the midst of this. He's promising you that you can trust Him even when it all feels like more than you can bear.

So instead of trying to pull you out, I'm lifting you up. I'm kneeling before the Father, and I'm asking Him to give you strength. To give you hope. I'm asking Him to protect you and to move you when the time is right. I'm asking Him to help you stay prayerful and discerning. I'm asking Him how I can best love you, and be a help to you. I believe that He's going to use your life in powerful and beautiful ways. Ways that will leave your heart grateful and humbly thankful for this road you've been on."

Kimberly Henderson - Proverbs 31 Ministries

Close your eyes for a minute and imagine you are in a rowboat. When you first set out to row across the lake, the water was calm, and the sun shone warmly on your back. It was peaceful in your little boat, but now the wind has picked up, and the waves are tugging against your oars. You have to dig deep and pull hard to continue to make headway across the lake. You can't go back, it's too far, but you have no idea how far it is to the other side either because your back is to the opposite shore, and the way is shrouded in a heavy fog. If you give up now, you will be adrift at the mercy of the waves and current, but if you keep going, you never know; you may be just metres from the shore. For all you know, a breakthrough might be just around the corner—a new opportunity, a change of circumstances, so don't give up under pressure.

Chapter 4

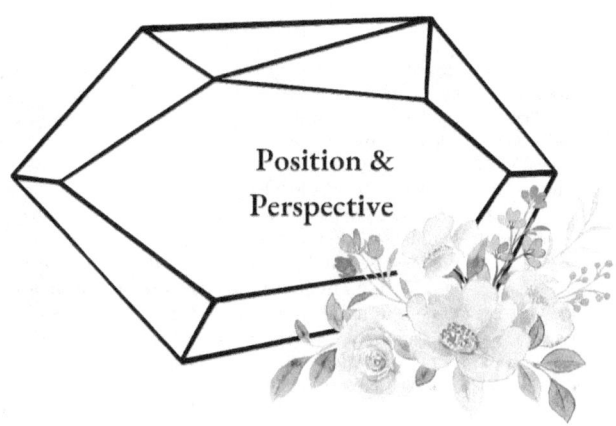

Position & Perspective

Sometimes God positions us where He needs us to be, but other times we need to position ourselves. We may have a dream but have no idea how we are going to get there. When it looks impossible it is likely to be a 'God' dream—something bigger than anything we believe we could ever achieve! The first step is trusting God with that dream. If we truly believe He placed it on our heart then we need to first surrender the timing and the outcome to God, but then there are certain steps we can take to position ourselves to receive it. That may be a position of prayer—down on our knees in surrender, petitioning God for what it is we desire. Or it may be stepping out in faith to do what we know to do. Obedience to what God has asked of us in the present season will position us for the next season when God begins to reveal His plans for us. When we don't know how to get there, we should find something that we CAN do, and DO THAT. It should be something that helps to narrow the gap between where we are, and where we want to be. It may be getting some training, or sowing into an area that relates to what we want to do. God will honour that.

CHAPTER 4 - POSITION AND PERSPECTIVE

"Perspective depends not only on what you look at, but also on where you look from."

— *JAMES DEACON*

Position:

1. Condition with reference to place; location; situation.
2. A place occupied or to be occupied; site: a fortified position.
3. The proper, appropriate, or usual place: out of position.
4. Situation or condition, especially with relation to favourable or unfavourable circumstances: to be in an awkward position; to bargain from a position of strength.

5. Status or standing: He has a position to maintain in the community.
6. High standing, as in society; important status: a person of wealth and position.
7. A post of employment: a position in a bank.
8. Manner of being placed, disposed, or arranged: the relative position of the hands of a clock.

Perspective:

1. The state of existing in space before the eye.
2. The state of one's ideas, the facts known to one.
3. A mental view or prospect.

To take a position on an issue means to have a strong opinion on something. Your opinions are generally based on your perspective, so you see that position plays a huge part in perspective, doesn't it? Some people see the glass as half full, while others see it as half empty. So many things shape our perspective on life. Our upbringing, where we were born, our culture, race, social standing, and our position within our employment. The list could go on. We all see the world through a different lens—that's called worldview. The lens by which we view the world. We just can't escape it. Our position will impact our perspective and vice versa. The guy in the ditch will give you his opinion based on where he is standing. It's dark, wet, and slippery. The guy standing on the road in the hot sun will tell you something completely different. The person who was raised in the slums of South Africa will have a hugely different worldview than the person born and raised in upperclass New York. This is what God has to work with when dealing with people. Perspective is not just about seeing with the eyes, it's also about how we think. He gave us all freedom of thought. He knows that we will not all see things the same way. So what's the answer? While He has given us this freedom, He knows that to have a heavenly perspective—to see things as He does will give us far more freedom and success than anything we could come up with ourselves. The Bible teaches us all about having a heavenly perspective. Jesus demonstrated this in the way He lived. We have a choice whether we will take on this perspective or not. That's the free will God has given us. If we choose to surrender to His superior plan, He will take us through a process; the transforming process of renewing our minds, as it states in Romans 12:2: (TPT) *"Stop imitating the ideals and opinions of the culture around you, but be inwardly transformed by the Holy Spirit through a total reformation of how you think. This will empower you to discern God's will as you live a beautiful life, satisfying and perfect in his eyes."*

What we look for is what we will see. If we are focussed on seeing the beauty in the world around us, then that is what we will find. However, if we are focussed on all the ugliness of the world around us, then that is what we will find. Have you ever noticed that if you decide you would like to buy a blue convertible, then from that point on, you will see them wherever you go. Recently I had the honour of decorating for a friend's wedding. She didn't want to spend a fortune on foliage for the decoration, so I figured I could source enough for free from around my neighbourhood. For the next month, everywhere I drove, my eyes were busy scanning the streets for foliage that I could possibly use without taking anything I shouldn't. Soon, I could not drive anywhere without being overly conscious of every tree and shrub along the way, to the point where it might have caused an accident because I was so distracted. I wasn't watching the road! But then one really good thing came out of it. I was suddenly aware of the beauty of creation all around me. I live in a suburb of the city—a concrete jungle, and I normally hate winter and think of it as very dull and bleak, but this opened my eyes to see the amazingly intricate beauty of the trees and shrubbery during the winter season right in my own backyard. It gave me a whole new perspective. I was quite surprised and delighted. It not only changed how I saw my surroundings with my physical eyes, but it also gave me a new appreciation for the season I was in. It altered my attitude; it brightened my mood. A change in perspective can do that.

There's a guy in the Bible that illustrates this well. His name is Joseph. He had a whole lot of brothers, but for some reason, his father favoured him above them all. It seems that Joseph was pretty proud and even a bit cocky about his favoured position. One day he had a dream, and his interpretation was that his brothers would all one day bow down to him. It might have been a good idea for him to keep that bit of information to himself, but being the young seventeen-year-old lad he was, he instead went and boasted about it to his brothers. So naturally, they were offended and decided to knock him down a few pegs. Unfortunately, they took their resentment to the extreme and decided to throw Joseph into a pit and then sold him off to some passing traders as a slave. Some of them even wanted to kill him off. Here is Joseph now in a very different position than he was only days before. They say pride comes before a fall. Well, that certainly was Joseph's experience! I imagine he was feeling a bit confused. Didn't he just have a dream that in the future, his brothers would all be bowing down to him. It didn't seem so likely from his new position down in that pit. Things would have looked rather bleak.

Have you ever dreamed of doing something and were feeling pretty optimistic until something happens to change your circumstances, and then it all starts to look pretty unlikely? It is easy to be optimistic when we're in a good position, but when circumstances are not optimal, it is much harder to have a positive outlook. When we're going through the process of transformation, we will likely experience this time and time again. God is interested in our response. He places us in certain positions in order to work on our perspective.

When you're having a bit of a pit experience, will you give up on your dreams? Will all you see be the dark slimy walls that encase you, or will you choose to hold on to a hopeful perspective by seeing past your circumstances to a brighter future beyond?

Joseph got out of that pit. So will you. He was dragged out of that pit and sold into slavery. Hmm. I can see the spiritual implications of this. Can you? Sometimes we get dragged out of the pit only to find ourselves enslaved to something. Not much of an improvement in circumstances! Let me give you an example to explain what I'm getting at.

Someone may hate their life—hate their circumstances, so they seek out some sort of pleasure to distract them from the pain they are feeling. They might drown their sorrows in alcohol or take drugs. Or some people like a bit of retail therapy, which then gets out of hand and lands them in debt. That's slavery. It might pull them out of their despair, but it will land them back into slavery to addictive habits. Maybe they need to stay put for a while. They might even be right where they need to be for the time being. Perhaps Joseph was in that pit for a good reason. As unpleasant as it was, I think Joseph learned some humility from his change in position. Was God preparing him for something in the future? Was God preparing him to be able to handle the very dream that landed him in that pit in the first place? Let's see what happens next.

Joseph must've thought he'd made it. He had been promoted from slave to head of Potiphar's household. A most coveted position. Potiphar obviously recognised something in Joseph worthy of the promotion. The Bible tells us that God gave Joseph success in everything he did. This was what Potiphar saw in him. But then, before he knew it, he found himself in prison through no fault of his own. Joseph did everything right. When Potiphar's wife set her sights on Joseph when she attempted to lure him into her bed, he did everything within his power to do the right thing, yet he could not avoid a bad outcome. What a shock that must have been? My first thought was, "hang on a minute, wasn't God supposed to be giving him success in everything he did." It doesn't look much like it now, does it? He resisted temptation, and yet he still got himself into trouble. That doesn't seem fair. Why would God allow it?

Gods' ways are not our ways. God had bigger and better plans—something with more far-reaching influence. Something that Joseph could never achieve in the position he had been in previously. God had to reposition him, and in doing so, He also adjusted his perspective. His motives changed too. Joseph had to go through the valley to gain a better perspective. We discover things in the valley that we don't see when we are on the mountain, and vice versa. The valley experience can bring us to a place of new insight and understanding. It can alter our perceptions of the world, our view of God, and lead us to change. We have all been through these valley experiences. Psalm 23 talks about the "valley of the shadow of death". In the valley, it can feel like everything is spiritually or emotionally dry or dead. You might even feel like you just wish you could die and go to Heaven. Psalm 84:6a (TPT) describes it as the "valley of weeping or tears". *"Even when their paths wind through the dark valley of tears..."* It doesn't sound like anywhere I want to be! Yet it is important for us to go through valley experiences—times of hardship and sorrow. Why? We talked about this in the previous chapter, but let's see what we can glean from Psalm 84:4-7. I'm going to dissect this passage into chunks so that we can find all the little nuggets of revelation.

VERSE 4: *"What joy for those whose strength comes from the Lord, who have set their minds on a pilgrimage to Jerusalem.* The dictionary describes a pilgrimage as, **"a journey, especially a long one, made to some sacred place as an act of religious devotion. It's any long journey, especially one undertaken as a quest or for a votive purpose, as to pay homage."** In this passage, it is talking about travelling to Jerusalem. Jerusalem is a holy and sacred place. Not only that, it is set on a hill. We can have joy in the valley experience by drawing our strength from the Lord. Jerusalem was set on a high hill. We will make it through the valley and reach higher ground if we set our minds on the destination rather than on our 'valley experiences'. In Colossians 3:2 it tells us to set our minds on the things which are above, or as it says in The Passion Translation, *"... feast on all the treasures of the heavenly realm and fill your thoughts with heavenly realities, and not with the distractions of the natural realm.."*

Going back to Psalm 84 and in verse 6, (TPT), it says, *"Even when their paths wind through the dark valley of tears, they dig deep to find a pleasant pool where others find only pain..."* When God positions us in the valley, we can choose to see things at a surface level, or we can dig deep into the Word—into the things of God. We can allow God to dig into the deep places of our hearts to draw out and expose anything or any place that needs to be restored within our souls. That is when we discover *"pleasant pools or refreshing springs"* (NLT). Where others would only find pain, those who dig for it will find refreshment and restoration.

"He gives to them a brook of blessing filled from the rain of an outpouring." Verse 6b (TPT) The valley experience positions us for blessing. It is in those difficult valley times that I often have an encounter with the Lord. In the valley, I find myself pressing into God—seeking his presence, relying on Him rather than on my own strength. Desperation sends me to my knees. As I press into Him and soak in His presence, He pours out his spirit on me. Then I feel so blessed. *"They will continue to grow stronger,*

and each of them will appear before God in Jerusalem." Verse 7 (NLT) *...these roads curve up the mountain, and at the last turn—Zion! God in full view!"* (MSG) Going through the valley strengthens and prepares us for the mountain-top experience. It is there that we learn the important lessons and develop the tenacity and strength of character that we need to bear the responsibility that comes with scaling new heights.

I long for that day. I feel as though I have been in the valley so long. But even as I type this statement, I feel as though I am right on the cusp of something amazing, and I am so ready! I can honestly say that God has changed my perspective during this valley experience I have been walking through. Now that I am almost at the other end, I know God is positioning me to move into the next season. I am sure the next season will have its challenges too, but I am excited to be moving on to a mountain-top experience. We all know that the mountain-top experience does not last forever, but it is just as an important part of the process of shaping and refining us as the valley experience. Deuteronomy 8:6-18 (NLT) *"So obey the commands of the Lord your God by walking in his ways and fearing him. For the Lord your God is bringing you into a good land of flowing streams and pools of water, with fountains and springs that gush out in the valleys and hills. It is a land of wheat and barley; of grapevines, fig trees, and pomegranates; of olive oil and honey. It is a land where food is plentiful and nothing is lacking. It is a land where iron is as common as* *stone, and copper is abundant in the hills.* **When you have eaten your fill, be sure to praise the Lord your God for the good land He has given you.** *"But that is the time to be careful! Beware that in your plenty you do not forget the Lord your God and disobey his commands, regulations, and decrees that I am giving you today. For when you have become full and prosperous and have built fine homes to live in, and when your flocks and herds have become very large and your silver and gold have multiplied along with everything else, be careful! Do not become proud at that time and forget the Lord your God, who rescued you from slavery in the land of Egypt. Do not forget that He led you through the great and terrifying wilderness with its poisonous snakes and scorpions, where it was so hot and dry. He gave you water from the rock! He fed you with manna in the wilderness, a food unknown to your ancestors.* **He did this to humble you and test you for your own good. He did all this so you would never say to yourself, 'I have achieved this wealth with my own strength and energy.' Remember the Lord your God. He is the one who gives you power to be successful, in order to fulfil the covenant He confirmed to your ancestors with an oath."*

When everything is going well, the danger is that we become too comfortable and complacent. We begin to rely on our own strength, and we forget that our success comes from God. From our mountain-top position, we can think we are invincible, like we've got it all together and don't need anyone else. From this high point, we can see clearly for miles around. It's great to have a broad perspective, but we need to remember that God alone can see the whole story from beginning to end. He sees the bigger picture.

The other danger with being in the mountain-top position is that we can become proud and start to look down on other people who are positioned in the valley. We might, for example, think, "I'm up here because I am a good person. I am superior, and that's why God has positioned me in this way." Joseph might have been tempted to think that way; in fact, I think that's the kind of sense of entitlement he would have had in the beginning before God quite literally gave him a change of perspective—the bottom of a dark hole. Fortunately, God did not leave him there. He soon found himself running the Potiphar's household, but just when things were looking up, he had another change in position and perspective, from thinking that it was all about him, to sitting in a smelly prison cell where he began to understand that he existed for more than his own pleasure. Previously, the dream was all about him. When Joseph was in the pit after his brothers threw him in there, his greatest desire would have been for someone to save him. But a little time in another dark hole changed it from being all about saving his own skin, to saving all of God's people. God's positioning of Joseph in the pit, then within Potiphar's' house, then later in prison, and finally as Pharaoh's second in command was a whole process that led to the salvation of the Israelites.

Through all the ups and downs of your life, God is positioning you just where he needs you in order to fulfil his plans and purposes. If God promoted you prematurely, there is a danger you would be ill-equipped to handle that more prominent position. We can trust God to know how much we can bear.

God wants to polish you until his reflection shines back at him. Jesus spoke and acted with great authority, and yet he was a most humble man. Humility is not about being in a low position but rather being in a lofty one yet recognising that you are not there through your own merit. The same applies if you are in a lowly position you can still act and speak with authority because you know your identity is not in your position but rather it is in the one whose image you bear and more and more so as you surrender to his refining and transformational process.

There is one more position I want to talk about. Between the valley and the mountain is the position of transition. I am pretty sure that's where I am right now. I have been praying that God would begin to open doors for me into a new season. I have been a stay-at-home mother and home educator for a very long time. Next year my youngest child will be moving on to tertiary education, and so that season of my life will come to an end. I'm already feeling the pressure of trying to figure out what is next for me. I had a dream the other night. It seemed I was at an airport getting ready to depart. I went through a doorway. It was a glass sliding door that immediately closed behind me. I found myself in a kind of holding space. There was another identical door in front of me, but I could not go through it because I didn't have the right key card, but neither could I retreat through the previous door to seek out help. I was trapped in there and began to feel a bit panicked. It wasn't very long before someone appeared and handed me the right key card so I could enter the doorway in front of me. It wasn't difficult to interpret what the Lord was communicating to me through this dream. I am in a position where I can't go back, but neither can I move forward. I am waiting for God to give me the keys to open the door to my next season.

Being in transition is uncomfortable. We know we can't go back to the way things were. God has been preparing us for something new, and we may likely feel it within our spirit— a kind of spiritual restlessness, urgency, or expectancy. It is like when a full-term baby is engaged in the right position, ready to be birthed. (Funnily enough, the final stage of giving birth is called the transition.) As uncomfortable as it is, it is an exciting time. No one enjoys the unknown—not knowing quite what to expect. I am not only spiritually stuck in a 'holding' space at the moment but also physically. Here in Auckland, we have been in level 4 lockdown due to Covid 19 for the past month and will likely be here for a while yet. Some days I feel a bit like a caged lion. God is teaching me to live in the present by taking each day as it comes. I ask God in the morning what He wants me to do today. I know it is only a matter of time before I will be released into all that God has prepared for me.

On another note on the topic of perspective. In another dream I had lately I was in a tunnel— it had a channel of water going down through the middle. I was on a small vessel that was more like a surfboard than a boat. All of a sudden, a large cruise ship entered the tunnel and came alongside me, completely dwarfing my little vessel. I was worried it was going to squash me against the side of the tunnel wall, but it just scraped by. A second time it bumped me against the sides, but I was okay. Then the third and final time it bumped into me and sent the 'surfboard' sinking straight to the bottom. The ship then squeezed through a narrow shaft and was docked in the ocean outside the tunnel. After praying and giving it some thought, I realised that the tunnel was like a birthing canal. Boats represent ministries. Small boat - small ministry. A large cruise ship represents a large ministry involving lot's of people. The surfboard spoke of my area of ministry now, and the large ship represents the ministry God is going to birth for me in the future. The new ministry will dwarf the ministry I have now in comparison. Like it says in the Bible. "If you are faithful in little things, you will be faithful in large ones." And in

Ephesians 3:20 (TPT) where it says, *"Never doubt God's mighty power to work in you and accomplish all this. He will achieve infinitely more than your greatest request, your most unbelievable dream, and exceed your wildest imagination! He will outdo them all, for his miraculous power constantly energises you."*

My first thought when I woke up was that this dream was a warning that something bad was going to happen. But after I prayed and asked the Holy Spirit for an interpretation, He gave me a whole new perspective. Now what I am getting at as far as perspective goes is this. I could have thought, "yikes, that huge ship blew my little vessel out of the water! That's sad. But after seeking the Holy Spirit for His perspective, I realised He was saying something entirely different. He was saying that He is getting ready to birth me into something new—to entrust me with something far greater than before because of my faithfulness all these years in the seemingly small.

Learning to live with the Corona virus has been difficult these past two years. It has turned our lives upside down. Here in New Zealand, we have been under level 4 lockdown. This is very restrictive. It means we can only go outside of our homes to go for a short walk around our neighbourhood, and only one member of the family is permitted to go to the local supermarket to buy groceries. Now there are two ways we could look at this. On the one hand, I could feel like I am in a kind of prison with many restrictions. I mentioned earlier that this time last week, I was feeling like a caged lion, and my roar could be heard throughout the house. When mamma ain't happy, ain't nobody happy! But in my better moments, I have a more positive mindset. I like to think of this time as an incubation period rather than a lockdown. Or think of it as a time of metamorphosis. We can choose our perspective, and this will determine what we do with our time. I am choosing to press into God and to use my creativity to accomplish projects around the home that I normally wouldn't have time for. It has also given me time to get stuck into writing this book. Before lockdown, I was lucky to spend an hour a week writing, if that!

As I said, I feel that I am in a time of transition. Only a couple of weeks ago, I received some news that shook me up a bit. I started to feel some apprehension about the future. It took me a few days to process those feelings. In actual fact, my feelings and mindset went through a transition of their own. Dr Caroline Leaf describes this as a reconceptualisation—seeing things from a different angle, or redesigning a thought. (DrLeaf.com "5 Simple and Effective Mental Self-Care Tips Guaranteed to Reduce Anxiety in Your Life and Boost Brain Health".) She says that you have a choice about how to see a situation or experience it. You can give yourself a new way of understanding it. In thinking about my future, I was actually looking back at my past and projecting former experiences and feelings onto my thoughts about what the future would hold. First of all, just let me say, don't let your past dictate your future. After having had time to process, I realised what I was doing. I needed to repent of that and ask God for His perspective. I needed to reconceptualise. Dr Leaf states that "as you start looking at this situation or experience differently, all the chemicals, hormones etc. start flowing differently, and actually change the physical structure of that thought." Instead of feeling anxious about the changes that were ahead of me, I began to get excited. This next season of my life could be an opportunity for God to do something great.

I am now going to walk you through a little exercise that will hopefully help give you some revelation about what God is doing in your life. All you need is a pen or several coloured pens if you prefer, and a piece of blank paper. Now promise me that you won't read ahead until you have done this, or it won't work. You need to follow the steps without knowing anything about why you are doing it until you've finished. Also, just one thing, don't worry about being artistic. Stick drawings are more than adequate for this exercise. You don't need to be a skilled artist! So here goes.

Step One: Draw a bridge in the centre of your page, leaving space around the outside of the paper for the next step.

Step Two: Now, draw what you see on either side of the bridge.

Step Three: Add in any extra little details you want to add to your scene. Is there anything above or below, for example?

Step Four: Now, place yourself into the scene. Where are you? A small dot or stick figure to represent yourself is fine.

Now it is time to analyse your drawing. Ask the Holy Spirit to give you insight into His perspective.

Here is what I drew when I did this little exercise before I knew what it was all about.

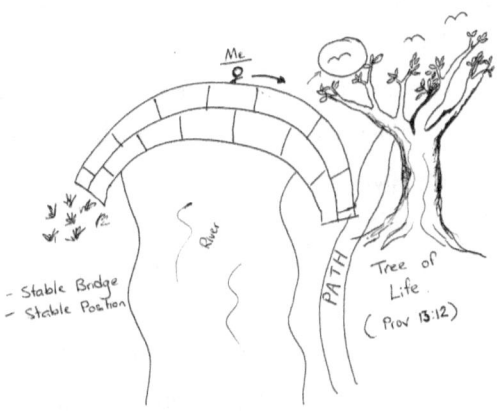

And here is what I felt the Lord say to me.

The bridge represents transition. I am facing the right side. That is the new season that God is moving me into. Last week I was thinking about the verse which says, *"hope deferred makes the heart sick, but when a longing is fulfilled it is a tree of LIFE.* (Proverbs 13:12) My longing is for God to move me forward out of transition into a new ministry involving many people. I drew the tree on the right first and then the grass on the left was an afterthought, or so I thought, but afterwards, I realised that it was also significant. Grass grows much smaller than trees. Trees are large and look a lot more majestic, but they are both living and also life-giving things. God showed me that the season I am leaving behind, namely home schooling and raising my kids for the past 21 years, is no less significant than my desire to have a ministry in speaking to women. It looks more exciting and honourable but it isn't. He reminded me not to undervalue what I have been faithfully doing in the past season of my life. I believe that is why the transition period is so important. It gives us perspective. It allows us time to reflect on the past season with fresh eyes because it's harder to see things clearly when you're still in it up to your eyeballs. And it also allows you time to seek God for revelation about the next season. He won't show you everything. That would just spoil the excitement when the time comes! But He will give you a glimpse if you seek Him for one—if you allow Him to give you His perspective to look into the future with hope and expectation.

In step four, my first instinct was to place myself in the middle of the bridge, but then I changed my mind and circled the bird in the sky. That represents the longing of my heart to fly as in Isaiah 40:31- *"but those who hope in the*

LORD will renew their strength. They will soar on wings like eagles..." But on second thought, I decided that placing myself on the bridge was a more accurate representation of where I was at present. It was then that it dawned on me that the bridge represents transition. The bridge is sturdy and strong. It is not a bad place to be. Standing on a firm foundation. The water represents the living waters of the Holy Spirit. And finally, the path. I actually had to stop and ask the Holy Spirit what that was about right here as I am writing this. He led me to this scripture in Psalm 16:11 (TPT) *"Because of you, I know the path of life, as I taste the fullness of joy in your presence. At your right side I experience divine pleasures forevermore!"* I don't have to know where the path leads. In the picture, the path fades into the distance. I can trust God that He will guide me down the right path when the time is right to move ahead. I don't need to be able to see where it leads. I can trust God with the future.

Learning to have a kingdom perspective during a time of transition is very important. It can mean the difference between a dream dying or being fulfilled! Take the Israelites, for example. They were in a place of transition between being set free from slavery in Egypt and entering into the land God had promised would be theirs. God told Moses back in Exodus 3:8 (NIV) that He was bringing them out of Egypt into *"a good and spacious land, a land filled with milk and honey."* So when Moses sent the ten spies into the land, he already knew this.

When they returned, they confirmed that, indeed it was a land flowing with milk and honey just as God had said. However, they were spiritually short-sighted! Their report was based on what they saw with their physical eyes. Caleb and Joshua saw the same things but had a very different attitude. They were all for moving forward into the promised land despite the obstacles. Their perspective was not based on fear but rather upon faith. God has promised this land so let's go and possess it. The eight other spies stirred up fear within their community. Fear spreads easily. God did not reward their fearful attitude, but rather, He rewarded Caleb for his faith. *"I was forty years old when Moses, the servant of the Lord, sent me from Kadesh-barnea to explore the land of Canaan. I returned and gave an honest report, but my brothers who went with me frightened the people from entering the Promised Land. For my part, I wholeheartedly followed the Lord my God. So that day Moses solemnly promised me, 'The land of Canaan on which you were just walking will be your grant of land and that of your descendants forever, because you wholeheartedly followed the Lord my God.'"* Joshua 14:7-9 (NLT)

What can we learn from this? If God has promised us something, then we can be confident that He will make a way for us to receive it. There is a danger in focusing on the difficulties that we are facing rather than on what God has promised. If we focus on the impossibilities, we may never reach our destiny. The Bible says that *"If you are able to believe, all things are possible to the believer."* Mark 9:23 (TPT)

We can't move forward while all we can see are the obstacles. Here's a little example. At the beginning of the year, one of my goals was to save $10,000.00 or more to convert part of our garage into a front entrance and lounge. At that time, I had no idea how I would ever be able to save that kind of money. We had never done it before. I didn't know how but I wrote it down and began declaring my goal every day and thanking God for making a way. Now I could have said to myself, "there's no way we are going to be able to do this." In fact, by September, we were in the middle of a lockdown due to the Covid pandemic and were not able to mix with anyone outside our bubble. Framing timber was in short supply. The guy we thought could help us build the project on the cheap, was unable to do it. I couldn't even go shopping for supplies except online. It all seemed impossible. But I kept believing, declaring, and thanking God. Money came in from unexpected places. For Example, mid-year, I received an unexpected payment of $4,500.00 from Inland Revenue! We were almost halfway there! In the end, we were able to ask my young nephew, a builders apprentice, to help. He had all the necessary tools and skills. Because he was family, he was allowed into our bubble. My son was working at a hardware store and was able to get us a major discount on much of, if not all, of the building supplies. I was able to purchase all the doors and windows secondhand online. A close friend who owns a moving company picked up all the supplies in her truck free of charge. We finished the project just three days before Christmas!

During the time of process that God takes us through towards the special assignments He has for us, He will position us right where we need to be. It often doesn't make sense to us, but we just need to embrace it. God's ways are not our ways. From the position He places us in, He will then begin to adjust our perspective, giving us eyes to see as He does. God knows that if we try to take things on with an Earthly perspective that, we will most likely fail in our endeavour or end up hurting people along the way. Allow God to position you where He needs you to be and to give you a Kingdom perspective.

Chapter 5

Prayer is asking God for what you need. More than that; it's a conversation with Him about anything and everything that's on your heart. You certainly don't need to be on your knees to do it, nor do you have to close your eyes. Prayer is an ongoing conversation. Sometimes whispered. Sometimes shouted. Most often silently spoken within our thoughts. Sometimes poured out in combination with tears and anguish, and occasionally expressed with utter joy and jubilation! There really aren't any rules, just some guidelines. However you want to talk to God, that's up to you. Just make it a daily practice. Get in tune with God. If something is worrying you, get it off your chest. Lay it down. Let God take care of it.

Prophecy on the other hand is more about speaking something that is not yet necessarily a present reality, as though it already were. I love that little statement in the story about Gideon where the angel of the Lord said to him, "Mighty hero, the Lord is with you!" (Judges 6:12 NLT) Huh! Mighty hero is certainly a prophetic statement. At that point in Gideon's life he felt anything but mighty and to call him a hero was a stretch of the imagination by any definition! Yet, it is impossible for God to lie. It was not true yet, but God knows the future. In the Kingdom realm time doesn't exist. These words were spoken in truth, just not the present truth as we understand it in an earthly sense, but they would become true. Gideon just didn't know it yet. When God speaks prophetically over us we should begin to walk in that truth even if it is just with a new attitude of heart.

CHAPTER 5 - PRAYER AND PROPHECY

"Your words are powerful, they have prophetic implications. SPEAK LIFE."

— *@BUKYOJELABI*

Prayer:

1. A devout petition to God.
2. A spiritual communion with God, as in supplication, thanksgiving, adoration, or confession.

Prophecy:

1. The foretelling or prediction of what is to come.
2. Something that is declared by a prophet,

especially a divinely inspired prediction, instruction, or exhortation.

3. **A divinely inspired utterance or revelation: oracular prophecies.**
4. **The action, function, or faculty of a prophet.**

Prayer becomes a priority when the going gets tough! I remember the first significant prayer I ever prayed. Well, other than when I prayed the salvation prayer at age seven. I was in a boarding school for missionary children in Papua New Guinea. I was only eight years old at the time.

As you can imagine, being separated from my parents at such a young age was a difficult time in my life.. My simple, heartfelt petition to God was for a roommate my age. The boarding school was actually called a hostel. It was specifically for missionary children, and it wasn't like the large boarding schools that you are probably more familiar with. The hostel was designed in the shape of a 'U', with the girls' rooms on one side and the boys' rooms on the other, with the kitchen, dining area, and living room located in between. There were only about four or five rooms per gender. My room consisted of only two beds. My roommate at the time was four years older than me—almost considered a teenager. She was the closest to my age at the time. She already had a well-established circle of friends when I arrived, and so I was lonely. Not only was I away from my parents, but I also didn't have anyone to play with. I don't remember the prayer, but I certainly remember when it was answered. I can still visualise myself standing in the shower one evening before bed. It was the day we had a new arrival at the hostel—a girl my age who was to be my new roommate. Her name was Sarah, and she was the source of my celebration as I sang a song of thanksgiving to God for answering my prayer. I still remember the words. It was the first song I ever wrote. Just one month since I began to ask, God answered. Sarah and I became fast friends!

Since then, many of my prayers have been answered with a significantly longer delay. I believe that one reason is that as we mature as Christians, God wants to develop our faith. We won't mature if we get everything we want right when we want it. We have to develop our spiritual muscles and learn some perseverance.

It goes without saying that if we want to realise the potential that God has placed in us, then prayer will be an essential component. We have to talk to God. He is the source of the potential and the one who designed us for greatness in the first place. Prayer is all about aligning our desires with God's will. Just like a lump of clay will never shape itself into a stunningly formed pot or vase without submitting itself to the expert hands of the potter, neither will we fully become what we were created to be without first surrendering our will to God.

He places goals, dreams, and visions in our heart. He is the ultimate dreamer. His imagination transformed the "... soup of nothingness, a bottomless emptiness, an inky blackness..." (Genesis 1:1-2 MSG) into this wondrous masterpiece we call Earth and everything on it including you in all your splendiferousness! But it was never so that we would pursue only the dream, but rather, in the process of pursuing our dreams, we would learn to fully pursue the inspirer of dreams! Many have pursued their dreams and succeeded only to discover the cold hard truth: that the pursuit of success without a relationship with the one who ultimately gives us our purpose and meaning leaves an empty void. Instead of finding the happiness and contentment they thought would come with reaching their ultimate goal, they are still left wanting! Nothing can fill that void except God. Prayer is a vital part of our relationship with Him.

Prayer is also a way to process our thoughts and emotions. I am a person who likes to process by speaking out loud. Generally, I like to have someone I can talk to about what's going on internally, and by doing so I can usually come to a resolution even if the person I'm speaking with doesn't say a word. I even talk to myself out loud. It might look odd, but it helps me process information.

Similarly, prayer is a conversation with God. It may feel like a one-way conversation, but it is not. God knows everything. He has all the answers. He knows what we will say, but He wants us to come and talk to Him—to ask our questions, pour out our problems, and seek Him for answers. He could give us all the answers right away, but He likes having our attention. He wants us to be attentive, and He wants to be desired. It's all about relationship. That is why He created us, after all! Prayer pulls us closer to the heart of God and into intimacy with Him. God waits for us to draw Him into a conversation. Just like any close relationship, it will not be a happy, healthy one if we do not take the time to talk openly with each other. I know that there are times in my marriage when my husband and I see each other every day and talk to one another, but only on a shallow level. When the communication goes deeper passed everyday matters, I feel most connected with my spouse. In Psalm 103:7 we see that the people of Israel knew the deeds of God, they knew about Him, but Moses knew the character of God. He knew Him intimately. The Israelites only wanted God for what He could do for them. Then when the Lord came through for them, they turned away from Him, forgetting what He'd done. **Never let your desire for answered prayer become more important than your desire for a relationship with God.**

If there were no delay between the promise of something and its possession, we would never learn to pray. Why would we need to? We might throw up a quick request, but we would not learn to pray those robust, faith-filled prayers obtained only by working our way through the process— pushing against the resistance, not giving up or giving in— being persistent, enduring, and reaching towards our goal. God has good things for us, but we have to reach for them. He won't just put it in our hands. How much do we want it?

We live in a world where almost everything is instant. Instant coffee, TV on demand, and every bit of information we could ever require are just one Google search away. If we got everything we wanted as soon as we asked for it, we would take it for granted. We might even forget who it is that supplies all our needs. Our prayers would become a bit like putting money into a vending machine, pressing a button, and watching as our requests fall with a thud right into our hands. We would come to expect it! We should expect an answer to our prayers, but we shouldn't demand it or take it for granted when He does. The truth is, we don't deserve any of it. It's all unmerited. God's grace and favour—every blessing and answered prayer. We have done nothing to deserve it. We can be like spoilt children throwing a tantrum when we don't get our way! But any good parent knows not to give in to a tantrum! If they do, the child will learn that this behaviour is acceptable—that every time they want something all they have to do is throw a tantrum. Now having said that, while it's true that God does not want us to 'spit the dummy' when we want something, He does, however, desire us to be persistent. He wants us to be sure that what we are asking for is really important to us, important enough for us to persevere. So what might the difference be between throwing a tantrum and being persistent in prayer? A 'tantrum' prayer is when we complain, demand, and become impatient because God doesn't give us exactly what we want when we want it, whereas a persistent prayer is humble, consistent, and trusting; expecting that God is faithful to answer our prayers, but surrendering our will regarding how and when.

A delay in answered prayer also helps us to decide if what we are asking for is really what we need or was it just a passing whim? If you want something bad enough, you are usually willing to work for it. The Bible says, "ask and keep on asking." There's a passage in the Bible that talks about a man who bangs on his neighbour's door in the middle of the night, asking for food. At first, the neighbour tells him to go away and stop yelling and banging on his door in the middle of the night, but the guy is persistent. He won't go away. In the end, the neighbour gives in and gives him what he wants.

"So, it is with your prayers. Ask and you'll receive. Seek and you'll discover. Knock on heaven's door, and it will one day open for you. Every persistent person will get what he asks for. Every persistent seeker will discover what he needs. And everyone who knocks persistently will one day find an open door. Then Jesus gave this illustration: "Imagine what would happen if you were to go to one of your friends in the middle of the night, pound on his door, and shout, 'Please! Do you have

some food you can spare? A friend just arrived at my house unexpectedly, and I have nothing to serve him.' But your friend says, 'Why are you bothering me? The door's locked, and my family and I are all in bed. Do you expect me to get up and give you our food?' But listen—because of your shameless impudence, even though it's the middle of the night, your friend will get up out of his bed and give you all that you need." Luke 11:5-10 (TPT). When we pray persistently, it is not to remind God of our request but rather to remind ourselves who the source of all our needs is. It helps us focus on what is really important to God and us. Ask yourself, "is what I am asking for really important to me — to God, and am I willing to fight for it?"

A great example of this in the Bible is found in 1 Samuel 1:12-17 *"As she, (Hannah) was praying to the Lord, Eli watched her. Seeing her lips moving but hearing no sound, he thought she had been drinking. "Must you come here drunk?" he demanded. "Throw away your wine!" "Oh no, sir!" she replied. "I haven't been drinking wine or anything stronger. But I am very discouraged, and I was pouring out my heart to the Lord. Don't think I am a wicked woman! For I have been praying out of great anguish and sorrow." "In that case," Eli said, "go in peace! May the God of Israel grant the request you have asked of him.""* Hannah was praying so fervently that the priest watching her thought she was drunk! So deep in prayer was she that she didn't care who saw her or how she appeared to them. She was pouring her heart out to God. She was desperate and held nothing back in her intimate conversation with her Heavenly Father. She put it all on the line. Her passion and earnestness in asking for what she wanted were richly rewarded. Have you ever wanted something so desperately?

I remember when I was desperate for God to open the door for me to be involved in missions. As mentioned before, I had been to Vanuatu on a mission trip in 2009 and was anxious to return. It had been the highlight of my adult life since getting married and having my three children. For what seemed like an eternity, I prayed and prayed that God would make a way. I poured my heart out to God many times. I have journals full of my prayers and heartfelt petitions to God. I felt God had dangled a carrot in my face but was now keeping it at arm's length. My life, in the meantime, felt so mundane. I was focused on everything that was wrong with my life. I was depressed and desperate. That was a terrible time in my life, and I have no desire to return, but I can say with complete sincerity that the process God took me through during that time was invaluable, and I am so grateful that God used that time to stretch and transform me. Gradually the Holy Spirit began to shift my focus. I began to let go and trust God, but at the same time, I still hoped and prayed. I am so glad that I persevered in prayer. That time helped me to press into God like never before. It taught me to pray like never before, and it caused me to really take stock of my priorities. What was it worth to me? Was it selfish of me to ask God for this? Did God even want me to have the desire of my heart? Could I trust God with my heart's desires? God took me through a difficult but amazing discovery process, and slowly but surely, He began to answer my questions. I still don't have all the answers, but I know one thing: I can trust God. He eventually answered my prayers, and when He did, it was far better than anything I could have hoped.

It is a good idea to be clear and specific about our requests, but at the same time, we need to be flexible because God knows best. For example, in asking for a new car, I might pray like this. "God I really need a new vehicle that is large enough to fit our family and powerful enough to tow a caravan. You know how much I'd love to own a green Toyota with tinted windows and a roof rack. Having said that, Lord, if you have something even better for me or something better suited to our needs, then I pray Your will be done. Thank you that you know exactly what I need better than I know myself, and I trust you to provide me with what I need."

The cool thing is, sometimes our loving Father does make an exception. Sometimes he will surprise us and throw in a freebie—a bonus, something we barely even asked for, an extra blessing just to show us how much He adores us. For example, at the beginning of last year, I threw up a bit of a simple prayer to God. I said, "Lord I'm feeling bored and uninspired with my life. Would you open the door of opportunity for me to do something special—something just for me, something outside of my usual role of wife, mother, teacher, worship leader etc.? In this case, I wasn't specific. I didn't really know what I wanted, and I certainly didn't have to pray persistently for it. My prayer was probably more like, "God please answer my heart's desire, not fully knowing what exactly that was." And God spectacularly answered my prayer! I didn't even know how much I wanted it— needed it even until God provided the opportunity for me to go. He even provided the finance to make it possible, and He did it miraculously. I was given the opportunity to go to Vanuatu with a group of like-minded women to pass on our creative skills to the women in a poor community in Port Vila. A friend of mine posted something on Facebook about the trip, and when I saw it my heart leaped. "I would so love to do that, " I thought to myself, but I did not have the means to pay for my airfare and accommodation, so I stored the desire away. About a week later, the same friend contacted me about a project she wanted me to help her with. She would pay me to do the job, so she suggested that if money was the only reason I couldn't go on this trip, that would solve my problem. The minute I got off the phone I was Googling airfares to Vanuatu. I was so excited. Here was the answer to my prayers. Not only the trip to Vanuatu, but also the creative project for which my friend was paying me to do. I could hardly believe it! As a bonus, I found last-minute airfares at almost half the price the others who had already booked would had paid. I also began to spend hours seeking God for creative inspiration for the project I was being commissioned to do. It was all going so well.

Was the project going ahead? Long story short, she had't been able to obtain sponsorship for the project, and so much to our disappointment, it wasn't going to happen. This put me in a bit of a predicament. How was I to pay back my credit card debt for the trip? It was money I didn't have.

I felt a bit crushed. This was not the first time I had gotten excited about a project, only to find it was a dead end. Why would God dangle a carrot and then leave me high and dry? How could He let me spend all that money if He knew it wouldn't happen? A few weeks later, I received a phone call out of the blue from an associate saying that they felt led to give our family a monetary gift of what was a huge amount in our estimation! I was stunned, to say the least. Suddenly my blessings were abounding! God had orchestrated a miracle.

But as the date of my trip to Vanuatu approached, I realized I hadn't heard from my friend in a while.

I had been so confident that this project was God's will that I was confused as to why it didn't end up happening.

Although I was very disappointed that the project was not going ahead, at least God had provided the money I needed, and I still had the trip to look forward to. I ended up having the time of my life in Vanuatu.

It was everything I love: using my creativity to bless others, traveling to Vanuatu to hang out in the community with locals and not just as a tourist, having long conversations with my friend and roommate, hanging out and sharing stories with like-minded, purposeful women, and dining at seaside restaurants while sipping cocktails and watching gorgeous tropical sunsets. It was awesome!

That was an exciting time in my life. It happened just before the world went crazy due to the Corona virus. Now sitting here in lockdown, a good 20 months later, it has been a good reminder that God does answer my prayers. At the moment, it doesn't really feel like it! I'm feeling a bit stuck. It's worthwhile thinking back to instances like that when you are struggling. It helps bring perspective. I have been tempted to get down in the dumps lately because it feels like God is just not listening to my prayers! I know that He is, but I am frustrated and impatient for Him to act.

Be **SPECIFIC,**
Be **BOLD,**
Be Expectant,
But
Be **OPEN**
to God's superior plan.

Why does God delay answering our prayers? He is testing our faith. Do we really believe it? Do we have what it takes to keep believing and contending for what we need in prayer by faith? Is it really that important to us, or were we asking for the wrong reasons? It gives us time to sort out and clarify our deepest longings. God also uses this time of delay to prepare us. Are we asking too small? Maybe God wants to expand our faith to believe in something greater. As we discussed in a previous chapter, Joseph's prayer was for God to rescue him, but God had bigger and better ideas. He would not only rescue Joseph but all of Israel! What are you asking God for? Could it be that God has something far better in mind? Be specific, be bold, be expectant, but be open to God's superior plan.

I am learning that delay is okay. Delay is not a straight-out denial from God. He has good reasons to delay an answered prayer sometimes, and we can trust Him to know when to answer. But then there is also another reason for the delay. It may be that the enemy is causing a hindrance to your prayers.

In Daniel 10: 12-13 (NLT), we read an amazing account of an angel speaking with Daniel. *"Then he said, "Don't be afraid, Daniel. Since the first day you began to pray for understanding and to humble yourself before your God, your request has been heard in heaven. I have come in answer to your prayer. But for twenty-one days the spirit prince of the kingdom of Persia blocked my way. Then Michael, one of the archangels, came to help me, and I left him there with the spirit prince of the kingdom of Persia."* From this account, we can determine that resistance happens in the spirit realm, delaying our prayers' answers. Whatever the reason for the delay, we must remain steadfast in prayer if it is something we earnestly desire. If we believe that it is in line with God's will, we will have to contend for it. Keep praying and believing and make sure that what you confess with your mouth backs up what you believe. That's always a good test of what you truly believe. The Bible says that what is in our heart is most often what will come out of our mouth. Sometimes we might have to do it in reverse order. We declare it until we believe it. Our brain is a lot more likely to accept and believe what it hears coming from our own mouth rather than from anywhere else, so if you declare something enough, you will start to believe it.

Prayer doesn't have to be complicated. It is really just a conversation with God. Don't overthink it. Sometimes all it takes is a simple, heartfelt prayer. Let me give you an example. It was during my last mission trip to PNG in 2019 before Covid put a stop to any international travel. I had spent the day with the women's ministry teaching sewing and baking. It had been a long, hot day, and I was tired. One of my dear national friends came into the house and offered to help with all the dishes. While Eugenia scrubbed, she asked if I would pray for her. She explained that she had been experiencing pain in her lower abdomen and that the doctor had given a diagnosis, but she could not recall the name of the condition. It sounded like a repetitive urinary tract infection, so I offered her some apple cider vinegar which I knew to be helpful for such things. After laying hands on her and praying a simple but heartfelt prayer, I showed her how to take the vinegar with water and perhaps some honey or sugar to make it more palatable and then sent her on her way. I was busy putting away the dishes and thinking about how difficult life could be in Papua New Guinea, where healthcare is so lacking when Eugenia came running back inside, grinning from ear to ear. She had remembered what the doctor had diagnosed— cervical cancer! I gulped and forced a smile to cover my shock and horror! She smiled and went on her way. On the other hand, I ran into the bedroom and sobbed my heart out. "Lord, I feel so foolish. I wish I had more to offer my friend than a bottle of cider vinegar. I feel so useless." If I had known the diagnosis, I must confess that I would have been too afraid to pray for her. I heard The Lord say, "do you believe in the power of prayer or what? Is it not the best thing you could have offered her? When you prayed, did you have faith to believe for healing?" I had to admit He was right. If I could believe that my simple prayer would heal a UTI, why not cervical cancer? It has now been almost three years since I had any contact with my friend. I have no way of knowing if she is still alive. By faith, I believe that I will see her beautiful face smiling back at me once more when I return.

Prophecy is also an essential part of the process. When we are in that messy stage between claiming a promise of God and receiving the fullness of that promise, we may lose hope. We might start to question, "did God really say..., or am I really destined for such and such?" Receiving a Word from God may act as a reminder of God's specific promise to us, or it may also encourage us to persevere through the time of preparation that we are in. Because let's face it, waiting is not fun, and it's hard! In this in-between season, it's easy to lose clarity about what we have been called to do. It can also be easy to get discouraged or distracted. In Philippians 3:12-14 (TPT) There is a great description of how our life is like running a race, or I would describe it more accurately as a marathon. *"I admit that I haven't yet acquired the absolute fullness that I'm pursuing, but I run with passion into his abundance so that I may reach the purpose for which Christ*

Jesus laid hold of me to make me his own. I don't depend on my own strength to accomplish this; however I do have one compelling focus: I forget all of the past as I fasten my heart to the future instead. I run straight for the divine invitation of reaching the heavenly goal and gaining the victory- prize through the anointing of Jesus."

Receiving a prophetic word can be like getting a pep talk from God. Imagine you are in a marathon—yes, that's what it often feels like during the refining process. When you set out on this race, you were focused on the finishing line, you were excited and full of energy and enthusiasm, but somewhere in the middle of the race, you start to feel exhausted. Every muscle and bone cries out for you to give up. Just then, someone hands you a nice cold bottle of thirst-quenching water and runs alongside you for a minute, spurring you on. They spur you on by adjusting your focus from the pain you are feeling in this moment to looking forward towards the finish line. That's what a prophetic word does for us. If we are going to reach the absolute fulfilment of God's best for us—in our identity and the assignment God has given us—then we need encouragement to face forward and continue with perseverance and hope. We need to reignite the passion that we had when we set out on this 'race'. *"When there is no clear prophetic vision, people quickly wander astray. But when you follow the revelation of the Word, heaven's bliss fills your soul."* Proverbs 29:18 (TPT) We have to have a vision for where we are headed. We won't reach our full potential or realise our dreams unless we do. We need to be able to 'see' our victory and reach for it.

To be honest, I don't know the finer details of my assignment this next season, which I believe God is about to birth me into. I am finding that uncomfortable and disconcerting.

I want to know what to expect. I want details. I HATE WAITING!

Have you heard the phrase, "delay does not mean denial"? The more God takes me through the refining process, the more I understand that there are sometimes intense periods of waiting; times when we feel the pressure of God's transforming activity in our lives; times when it feels as though we are not moving forward, but that does not mean that God is denying our requests— our earnest prayers for transformation. Like I said, the details are still a little hazy, that's where faith and trust come in, but I do have a vision. I know that God has given me a message to share. I know that I want to speak into women's lives, and I want to use my creative talents. I don't fully know how God will package that, but I know I can trust Him with the details. I have received prophetic words and dreams that reveal what the future holds. I know God has good plans for me, so I don't need to fear or be anxious. Instead, I am expectant. I am beginning to imagine all the good things God has in store for me. Habakkuk 2:1-3 tells us that we should ..."*Write this. Write what you see. Write it out in big block letters so that it can be read on the run. This vision-message is a witness pointing to what's coming. It aches for the coming—it can hardly wait! And it doesn't lie. If it seems slow in coming, wait. It's on its way. It will come right on time."* It's important to record your vision. Get it straight in your mind and keep it somewhere where you can look at it and focus your thoughts and mind on it. In fact, I have taken it a step further. I have created a vision board so that I can see the things I am hoping for and working towards every day when I walk into my office. It helps me to focus forward and not dwell on the past.

While it is good for us to live in the present and be content, we need to be expectant for the future. It can be difficult when we get bogged down with the mundaneness of life not to start complaining. Prophecy can assist us in navigating the process. Rather than moaning about how things are, we can speak into the situation - prophecy over it. Don't tell it like it is; tell it like it could be because remember that "all things are possible to him who believes."

Words have great power. The Bible tells us that they have the power of life or death! We can choose to tell it how we see it—how it looks and feels in the moment from an earthly perspective, or we can tell it like we want it to be in accordance with what we believe God has promised. *"You will also declare a thing, And it will be established for you; So light will shine on your ways."* Job 22:28 (NKJV),

Also in Hebrews where it talks about faith. *"Now faith brings our hopes into reality and becomes the foundation needed to acquire the things we long for. It is all the evidence required to prove what is still unseen. This testimony of faith is what previous generations were commended for. Faith empowers us to see that the universe was created and beautifully coordinated by the power of God's words! He spoke and the invisible realm gave birth to all that is seen."* Hebrews 11:1-3 (TPT)

In the latter part of this passage, we see that God's words gave birth to all that is seen. With His words, He caused what was unseen to become visible and tangible. First, God had to imagine it, and then He had to speak it, and then it became a reality. If we follow this same example, is it unrealistic to think that perhaps the same principle applies to us? We are created in His image, after all! Jesus Himself said that we would do the same things as He did and even greater things will we do. (John 14:12) Therefore, I believe that on the basis of this principle and because our words have the power of life and death, I believe it is safe to say that we can put our faith into action with the words that we say. The Bible says that when we pray, *"Just make sure you ask empowered by confident faith without doubting that you will receive..."* James 1:6a (TPT). We can pray and ask God for what we desire, and if we truly believe, then we can also speak prophetically—declaring what is not yet visible as though it were. I might say something like, "thank you, Lord, that I am fit and healthy...by Your stripes, I am healed...I live in health and prosper even as my soul prospers". Even though I am still experiencing some health issues, I can thank God as though I were already healed.

Prophecy reveals God's perspective. When we receive a word of prophecy, we receive a revelation from the heart of God. It's something that God wants us to know about ourselves and our situation that we may not be able to see. Perhaps deep in our hearts, we know it to be true, but there is something about hearing it straight from the mouth of God. Prophecy has a way of drawing out our potential. There's a great passage in Judges that describes this. Gideon felt small and insignificant until God shows up in his life. An angel of the Lord appears to him and speaks prophetically over Gideon. He calls him a mighty warrior or a man of valour in some versions. The NLT even calls him a mighty hero! Gideon couldn't see beyond the position he was in at that moment. I often find myself doing the same thing.

When we are in the middle of the process towards something significant that God has called us to, we too can feel small and insignificant. We can easily get blinded by our circumstances, unable to see the potential that God wants to draw out of us. For example, as I've already mentioned, I have been a stay-at-home mum for 21 years. So many times, I have undervalued that role and felt small and insignificant. But God sees it differently. He sees greatness in me. When I receive a word from God, He tells me how he sees things not from an earthly perspective but from a kingdom one.

Gideon hasn't done anything to merit being called a hero. In fact, through human eyes, he looks more like a coward. But God is speaking in the present tense that which will be a reality in the future. Prophecy encourages us by giving us a glimpse into the unknown. It could be just around the corner, or years into the future, but it reveals what is to come if we allow God to continue working in us—if we surrender to the process.

Another helpful idea is that if you have any prophetic words recorded somewhere, you can turn them into a prayer or decree. The following is a prophetic word I received recently. I reconstructed it into a prayer. I added any verses that I thought of that applied to the prophecy so that I can declare it in confidence because it is the word of God and holds authority.

Prophetic word given on 4th of May 2021

The Lord wants to encourage you that there is more. He's asking you to lift your eyes because there's an abundance right above you, and it's almost like the angels are waiting, and they're just going to bring it. I don't know what you are doing, what you're involved with but there is more, and the Lord is saying receive it because the angels have got it right there – right there above you ready to bring it.

Fri 17th Sep 2021

God, I thank you for your encouragement to faithfully continue to do what I have been doing. I have been faithful in the small things, therefore, you are entrusting me with greater things. (Luke 16:10) There is more for me. Your power at work in me is accomplishing more than I could dare to hope or dream. (Ephesians 3:20) I will not grow weary in doing good for at just the right time I will reap a harvest of blessing if I don't give up." Galatians 6:9 (NLT) I need only to lift my eyes to the heavens—to shift my focus and set my mind on things above, not on earthly things (Colossians 3:2). There is an abundance right there waiting for me. Your servants, the angels are ready and willing to minister to me. (Hebrews 1:14) I see them coming down laden with blessings straight from the heart of God. Because I have faithfully offered myself as a living sacrifice, holy and pleasing to You as my act of true worship, (Romans 12:1) You will open the windows of heaven and pour out a blessing beyond my wildest imagination. (Malachi 3:10)

As wonderful as it is to receive a word of prophecy from the Lord, giving a word of prophetic encouragement to another is also rewarding. The Bible says that we are to earnestly SEEK the gift of prophecy. That doesn't mean that you are suddenly a prophet. No! To be considered a prophet is different from moving in the gift of prophecy. Any born- again believer can exercise the gift whether they are a prophet or not. A gift is just that; something given by God at any given time for believers to utilise as a means to build His kingdom.

In a recent zoom call I attended for training in the prophetic gift, we separated into breakout rooms to do an activation exercise called popcorn prophecy. It is called that because the word given has to be short and to the point. A group of about five people take turns to give a one-sentence prophecy to the person nominated to receive it. Each person adds on to the previous word given. After each person shares a prophetic word, another person is chosen as the recipient, and so on. At first, I was really nervous. Being rather a novice at the prophetic gift, I wasn't sure how or if I would be able to share a word.

On the first round, I waited until the last. I prayed in tongues and listened to the other words given and tried to tune in to the Holy Spirit. I wasn't confident, but I felt to say a word or two, and it wasn't till I spoke the first couple of words out loud that I received more to say. After it was out, I felt a bit shy and wondered if what I said was actually inspired by the Holy Spirit or whether I had made it all up somehow. But then the recipient of the prophecy responded that what I had said resonated with them and rang true. YAY! I thought. I'll give this another go. Well then, it was time for another person to receive a word. I found that a word of prophecy immediately began spilling out of my mouth. I was rather surprised and delighted! Where did that come from, I wondered? That was quite exciting and after the whole session was finished, I felt a huge sense of satisfaction and joy. It was quite rewarding to encourage a perfect stranger without relying on anything except the prompting of the Holy Spirit.

So why is this an important part of the process? Anything that encourages spiritual growth will be an important part of helping us to move from potential, to our destiny and help us to navigate that uncomfortable stage in between. The Bible says that it is better to give than to receive. If we desire prophetic revelation to encourage us and spur us on, we should also be prepared to give it. (1 Corinthians 14:1) As in my example above. In my own experience, sharing a word encouraged the recipient and boosted my confidence. It meant that as I shared what I thought I heard from God, what I heard was confirmed by the person I shared it with if indeed it resonated with them and they were encouraged. This helps us attune our spiritual ears to the voice of God so that when He gives us revelation about our calling, we can be more confident that we are indeed hearing the small, still voice of God and act accordingly.

Chapter 6

Patience and Perseverance

"Don't follow after the wicked ones or be jealous of their wealth. Don't think for a moment they're better off than you. They and their short-lived success will soon shrivel up and quickly fade away, like grass clippings in the hot sun. Keep trusting in the Lord and do what is right in his eyes. Fix your heart on the promises of God, and you will dwell in the land, feasting on his faithfulness. Find your delight and true pleasure in Yahweh, and he will give you what you desire the most. Give God the right to direct your life, and as you trust him along the way, you'll find he pulled it off perfectly! He will appear as your righteousness, as sure as the dawning of a new day. He will manifest as your justice, as sure and strong as the noonday sun. Quiet your heart in his presence and wait patiently for Yahweh. And don't think for a moment that the wicked, in their prosperity, are better off than you." Psalms 37:1-7 (TPT)

This passage of scripture is one that I have clung to during times of waiting in my life. While I'm waiting on God I am often tempted to compare my own situation with people who appear to have the kind of life and success that I dream of. This scripture tells us that this kind of success can be short-lived and quickly fade. That is not the kind of success I desire. When success comes to someone too easily, they do not develop the maturity or strength of character to be able to sustain it. Learning to be patient and to persevere through the process towards gaining our heart's desires will prepare us for when it comes to pass in God's perfect timing so that we have the strength to sustain it.

The root word of this word, 'wait' in Hebrew can mean "to whirl" or, "to be in labour". Different translations use such words as 'rest', 'be still', or as in the Passion Translation above, 'quiet your heart'. How can we 'be still' AND, 'whirl' or be 'as a women in labour'? It sounds like a contradiction. This kind of waiting requires us to remain in an attitude of trust, resting on God's faithfulness in His promises, but it will also require us to contend for what we believe. It is not a passive position but neither is it one of striving. It is holding strongly with earnest-ness, passion and zeal to that which God has promised, while trusting completely in God to bring it to pass in His perfect timing. The enemy will lie to us, to convince us that nothing is happening, that God is not working, and that we have to strive to make it happen. We will have to stand up and fight the battle going on within us. We will have to proactively silence the voice of the enemy and quiet our hearts with the truth of God's word.

CHAPTER 6 - PATIENCE AND PERSEVERANCE

"The hour of fulfilment is buried in years of patience."

— MARY OLIVER

Patience:

1. The quality of being patient, as the bearing of provocation, annoyance, misfortune, or pain, without complaint, loss of temper, irritation, or the like.
2. An ability or willingness to suppress restlessness or annoyance when confronted with delay .

Perseverance:

1. **Steady persistence in a course of action, a purpose, a state, etc., especially in spite of difficulties, obstacles, or discouragement.**

The main difference between patience and perseverance is that patience is the ability to endure difficult situations without being annoyed or anxious, but perseverance is the quality of continuing with something even though it is difficult. (pediaa.com)

Between a promise and its possession, there is nearly always a delay. I hate delays, don't you? Have you ever been excited to go on an overseas trip only to arrive at the airport to find the flight has been delayed? It's never fun to have to wait unless we decide to embrace the time in between by making the most of it. When we travelled when I was a little girl living with my missionary parents in Papua New Guinea, we were at the mercy of the seasons. There are only two seasons in the tropics—wet and dry seasons. At best, the roads were substandard, but during the dry season, we could get around ok. However, in the wet season, things could get rather difficult. We often got stuck in a particularly deep, boggy patch, and my father would have to get creative to get us out. He sometimes used snow chains on the tyres or placed logs or rocks in front of the wheels to give more traction. It could take us a while to move on in our journey, so we kids had to find a way to amuse ourselves while we waited. There is one particular incident I have never forgotten when my mother decided to help herself to a piece of timber from the cattle loading ramp in a nearby cattle yard. I guess she figured they wouldn't miss it! It still amuses me to this day.

The rivers were another issue. Back then, there were very few bridges. There were either low concrete ford, or otherwise, we would have to drive across the riverbeds. When it rained, the rivers flooded to dangerous levels. We would have to check the weather before deciding to go on our trip. At times we'd get caught out. We'd arrive at a river only to find the water was too high, so we'd WAIT...and WAIT...and WAIT! So how did we make the most of that time? Usually, swimming would be an option. Oh, how I loved to swim. It was always hot, so getting into the cool water was so refreshing, and I'd spend hours splashing around, but this wasn't an option if the river was flooded—too dangerous! So, we would settle down somewhere, and my mother or father would pass the hours by reading to us. I especially loved 'The Narnia Chronicles' and 'The Little House On The Prairie' series'. I remember those quiet moments of waiting with fondness. While we were waiting, my father would be vigilantly observing the conditions until he deemed it safe enough to attempt a crossing.

In the middle—in the delay—in the process between what is promised and its possession, we have two choices to make. Let's take a look at the Biblical account of Abraham to see how he responded to the process and how we can learn from this and apply it to our own lives. When God initially gave Abram (later re-named Abraham), the promise that he would be the father of many nations, he was seventy-five years old. After a decade of waiting for the promise to be fulfilled, Abram and his wife had grown impatient, so they decided to take matters into their own hands. *"Now Sarai, Abram's wife, had not been able to bear children for him. But she had an Egyptian servant named Hagar. So Sarai said to Abram, "The Lord has prevented me from having children. Go and sleep with my servant. Perhaps I can have children through her." And Abram agreed with Sarai's proposal."* Genesis 16:1-2 (NLT) *"So Hagar gave Abram a son, and Abram named him Ishmael. Abram was eighty-six years old when Ishmael was born."* Genesis 16:15-16 (NLT)

Who could blame Abram and Sarai for jumping the gun? A decade is a long time trying pregnant, when the parents are ancient!

WE CAN CHOOSE TO ACT PREMATURELY, OR WE CAN *Surrender* **TO THE PROCESS.**

Can you relate? Have you been waiting a long time for the fulfilment of a promise? I know I have.

We live in a world where most things are instant. People expect instant gratification. We don't like having to wait, but waiting is part of the process, and the process has an important role to play! Just as my dad was observant of the water and the weather before he made the call to continue our journey, so is our Heavenly Father always watching and observing the condition of our hearts to see if we are prepared to move ahead. That is why the process is important. It is preparing us for the next season. It strengthens us so that we are strong enough to possess what He has promised.

So, what are the two choices we have to make within the process? We can choose to act prematurely or surrender to the process. In the passages above, Abram and his wife became impatient and took matters into their own hands. The problem with doing that is there will always be consequences. Just like in the process of pregnancy, there is a process that needs to happen—the baby needs to develop fully within the womb before it is ready to be born. If the baby is born too soon before the due date, it will be premature, and under- developed. In Abram and Sarai's case, there were definite adverse consequences for their decision to get ahead of God's timing. (See Genesis 16:4-12)

In Genesis 17:17-19 (NLT) we see that Ishmael was not God's intended heir. Sometimes, we settle for second best in our impatience, and we forfeit God's best for our lives! Fortunately, God gives second chances. Even though Abram (now renamed Abraham) took matters into his own hands, God still gave him a legitimate son. God had a plan, and He gave Abraham a second chance at being part of it. *"Then Abraham bowed down to the ground, but he laughed to himself in disbelief. "How could I become a father at the age of 100?" he thought. "And how can Sarah have a baby when she is ninety years old?" So Abraham said to God, "May Ishmael live under your special blessing!" But God replied, "No —Sarah, your wife, will give birth to a son for you. You will name him Isaac, and I will confirm my covenant with him and his descendants as an everlasting covenant."*

So, what does it mean to surrender to the process? I learned this the hard way. There was a period when I was desperate for God to fulfil one of my dreams. As mentioned previously, I went on my first mission trip in 2009. It was a very special and impacting experience for me, but afterward, I was depressed. I wouldn't say clinically depressed, but there were days I just wanted to cry. I felt hopeless! I even remember saying to the Lord, "if this is how my life will be forever, then I would rather not live." I have since repented of this. I am well aware that the power of life and death is in the tongue, and I was convicted of my words! During the next few years of desperation, I gradually surrendered to the process. I learned to trust God with the outcome, let go of control, and trust in His perfect timing. Step one of surrendering to the process is letting go and trusting God. At first, I did everything I could think of to try and **make** things happen. Yes, I went down the road of taking things into my own hands, but every time I tried, it ended in another closed door and a lot of tears and frustration! That wasn't fun, I can tell you! I had to let go.

It took me a while to get to that point, but I felt so much better when I did. Gradually over time, I learned to surrender to God's perfect plan. I spent a lot of time in my secret place with the Lord crying and questioning Him. I journaled a lot too. I have been very sporadic with my journaling over the years, but when the going gets tough, that's when I seem to take it up again. It is a great way to hash things out with God and record the insights He gives you along the way. I love to look back on those journals from that dark period of my life to observe as a light began to switch on for me and grow steadily brighter. I can see God's hand working on my heart to bring me to that place of surrender and trust. My favourite journal ever is the one beginning in October 2009 and ending in December 2010. The time I was the most depressed. It is full of pages of pouring my heart out to the Lord, but not only that—it is full of God's promises and words of hope and encouragement to me. During that time, God gave me several scriptures to memorise, and I held on to those promises for dear life. They kept me afloat. One such entry in my diary from 2010 was a simple drawing of a stick figure floating around in deep water with various items floating around it. When I returned from my trip to Vanuatu in 2009, I wrote that I felt like I was set adrift—floating around just trying to keep my head above water. I couldn't get a solid footing. God spoke to me through scripture. 1 Peter 5:10 (NLT) says the following. *"In his kindness God called you to share in his eternal glory by means of Christ Jesus. So, after you have suffered a little while, He will restore, support, and strengthen you, and He will place you on a firm foundation."* As time went on, God did just that. Those scriptures gave me a solid foundation—something to hold on to; promises to stand firm upon. Another scripture He gave me was Habakkuk 2:3. (TLB) *"But these things I plan won't happen right away. Slowly, steadily, surely, the time approaches when the vision will be fulfilled. If it seems slow, do not despair, for these things will surely come to pass. Just be patient! They will not be overdue a single day!"*

Did that change my situation? No. But it did change my perspective. After I learned some patience and began to surrender to God's process, it became less painful to wait. Yes, life was still mundane, but I had hope. I believed God when He said in Jeremiah 29:11 that He had good plans for me. This gave me the ability to continue doing what I was doing even though it was tough. That's called perseverance! And that's where I find myself again right now. As I said, I feel that I am in a time of transition. That means I can't go back to life as it was, and I can't really step into the new until God gives the green light. I won't lie. Life is good, but it's feeling pretty mundane. Earlier I was tempted to feel a bit down and sorry for myself, but no! I shifted my focus which then shifted my attitude. The difference between now and back twelve or thirteen years ago is that I learned to surrender to the process. I went through everything I've been describing to you in the past five chapters. I lived it, which has prepared me for the season I am in now. Honestly, life is just a bunch of different seasons.

There is good and bad in every season, but each will grow us and prepare us for the next if we let it; if we allow God to do what He needs to do. So here I am, waiting and persevering. What does that look like for me? It means I am faithful to do what I can and what God has asked me to do, one of which is finishing this book and persevering through to getting it published. That kinda terrifies me, to be honest! I don't know if I can do it. I'm scared!

However, I am putting one foot in front of the other. The last couple of prophecies I received spoke of God's mercies being new every morning.

His provision of mercies is fresh every morning and sufficient for each day. I don't have to worry about tomorrow. I just have to be faithful to see out today with faith, patience, perseverance, hope and peace, knowing that tomorrow is taken care of!

If I sat here thinking about all of the things I'd like to do but can't do, I wouldn't focus on making the most of the opportunities I have. When I'm feeling a bit down, I know that I tend to withdraw and do nothing. Instead of feeling sorry for myself because my brother sold his holiday property up north, where we would normally spend our holidays and long weekends, I am making the most of any opportunity to get out and have a swim or do something fun even if it's just an hour or two. Sure, I'd love to plan my next annual mission's trip to Papua New Guinea right now, but due to an overzealous prime minister and Covid restrictions, that is not possible. Even a few years ago, that would have sent me into a pity party but not anymore. Over the past couple of years, I realise that God has been working. As the song says, 'even when I don't see it, you're working. Even when I don't feel it, you're working...'

Over the years, as my trust in God grew, I realised that God was the one who places the dreams and desires in my heart. He doesn't withhold things from us to taunt us and make us miserable, but rather to protect and prepare us.

Going back to the story from my childhood, as I said, while we were waiting, my father would constantly be observing the conditions before making a call as to whether we would go ahead and cross or whether it was too dangerous. There was always a very real danger that we could get swept away by the raging waters. I remember how I trusted my dad to convey us safely to the other side. Even when the water swirled in around my ankles, I was not fearful. We can trust our Heavenly Father in the same way. He is always vigilantly observing the conditions around us. He sees the dangers ahead and urges us not to move forward prematurely to our detriment but instead to trust in his perfect timing.

Isaiah 43:2 (NLT) *"When you go through deep waters, I will be with you. When you go through rivers of difficulty, you will not drown. When you walk through the fire, you will not be burned up; the flames will not consume you."*

Don't be in too much of a hurry. God is protecting and preparing us for the next season. When the timing is right— when the conditions are favourable and when God determines that we have the maturity to handle it, He will give us the green light. Doors will open for us, and we will not have to push too hard to make it happen. In the meantime, we should ask God for the patience to wait with a trusting heart and the perseverance to continue putting one foot in front of the other until He gives us the go-ahead to move into a specific promise, calling, assignment, or whatever we choose to call it.

"But that's not all! Even in times of trouble we have a joyful confidence, knowing that our pressures will develop in us patient endurance, (perseverance). And patient endurance will refine our character, and proven character leads us back to hope. And this hope is not a disappointing fantasy, because we can now experience the endless love of God cascading into our hearts through the Holy Spirit who lives in us!" Romans 5:3-5 (TPT)

Chapter 7

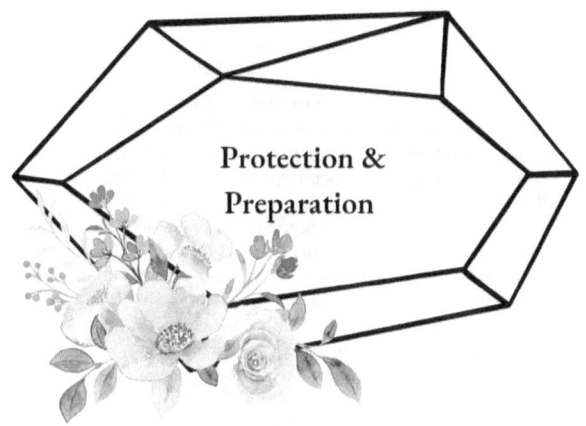

Protection & Preparation

Let's be honest. Waiting is not fun. I remember when I found out I was pregnant. I was so excited. But then came the long wait! If it had been down to me I would have hurried the process along quite a bit. But then my baby would have been born prematurely and would not have survived! The baby is in the womb for nine months for a reason. The longer they are in there, the more uncomfortable it gets for both mother and baby until one day it is time to give birth. But that discomfort is absolutely necessary. Baby needs time to fully develop and so do your dreams. We need time to move through the process described in this book in order to be ready when God says it's time. We need time to get into position; time to gain some perspective and determine our priorities; time to prepare and time to learn to praise God and proclaim who He is in all things, through the good times and the bad. Waiting for God's timing and embracing the process, prepares us, and protects us from giving birth to our dreams prematurely. God wants us to be fully prepared, equipped, and empowered to fulfil our destiny.

CHAPTER 7 - PROTECTION AND PREPARATION

"It is not often that a man can make opportunities for himself. But he can put himself in such shape that when or if the opportunities come, he is ready."

— *THEODORE ROOSEVELT*

Preparation:

1. A proceeding, measure, or provision by which one prepares for something: preparations for a journey.
2. Any proceeding, experience, or the like considered as a mode of preparing for the future.
3. An act of preparing.
4. The state of being prepared.

Protection:

1. **The act of protecting or the state of being protected; preservation from injury or harm.**

The in-between seasons are never wasted time. They are times of preparation. In my experience, God gives us dreams that are generally too big for us. He then spends time preparing us until we are better equipped to handle the responsibility that comes with the dream. By giving us time to grow and prepare, He is protecting us from getting in over our head!

When my children were young, I was a lot more protective of them. I did much more for them than I do now, and I expected less of them. As they have grown and matured, I am less protective and have eased off on controlling what they can and cannot do, and I expect more of them. I give them more responsibility and trust. I remember when my second child Ethan was only around three or four years old. We bought him a little plastic lawnmower. He liked to toddle around, pushing his mower behind his dad while he was cutting the grass on a Saturday afternoon. We would never have let him anywhere near the real mower because at that stage, Ethan was not tall enough or responsible enough nor anywhere physically strong enough to push it. Also, we couldn't trust him not to get his fingers or toes in the sharp blades, especially knowing what an inquisitive little guy he was! He loved to stick his fingers into things, pull things apart, and discover how things work. Of course, now that Ethan is over six feet and nearly twenty years old, he is expected to help out around the house. We now trust him with, and expect him to use the lawnmower. We even trusted him enough to do all the electrical work in our recent renovations.

It is the same with our Heavenly Father. As we develop and mature spiritually, He entrusts us with more Kingdom responsibility. Before giving us an assignment, He makes sure we are ready. We may not feel ready, and that's because if we could do it entirely in our own strength, then we wouldn't need to depend on God. Being ready is not necessarily about feeling good enough or competent enough. It may be more about having the right attitude or spiritual gifts. Only God can determine when we are ready for an assignment. When I refer to an assignment, I am talking about our calling or destiny, or a dream that God has placed in our hearts. Ephesians 2:10 is one scripture that describes this. I like to look at how different translations of the Bible express the same thing. In each version, we can usually glean some different insight. The Passion Translation says that. *"...Even before we were born, God planned in advance our destiny and the good works we would do to fulfil it!"* Here's how the Message translation puts it. *"...He creates each of us by Christ Jesus to join him in the work he does, the good work he has gotten ready for us to do, work we had better be doing."* The NLT describes it as *"...the good things He planned for us long ago."* However, you want to describe it, I believe that God has stuff that He wants us to do for the kingdom, and we each have unique roles based on our makeup—our personality, abilities, cultural background, talents, and spiritual gifts. God uniquely packages those attributes for a particular purpose for a time or season.

Part of being prepared is having a plan. As it says in the above verses, God planned the work we would do in advance. It is God who made the plan, and so we should therefore trust Him to bring it about, and in His timing. According to Proverbs 16:9 (MSG) *"We plan the way we want to live, but only God makes us able to live it."* It is better to follow God's plan than our own. That is not to say that we shouldn't have vision and focus. We need to have an idea of what God has called us to, but we don't have to have all the answers about how and when we will get there. When we surrender to God's process in our lives, we are demonstrating to God that He is in the driver's seat —that we are giving up control and trying to do things in our own strength, and are allowing Him to accomplish in us whatever it takes to prepare us for the responsibility of whatever it is He is entrusting us with and calling us into.

In a more practical sense, how does God prepare us? By firstly equipping us. Just like if we were going on a tramping trip in the jungle. There are certain things we would not survive without, like enough water, the right shoes, some sort of shelter, food is always good, lol, and maybe a map or compass. So, it is with our spiritual journey. As we work our way through the process of preparation, God is equipping us with such things as the fruit of the spirit, the gifts of the spirit, faith, maturity, and so on. If we step into a God-given assignment without this kind of 'equipment' we may not survive. Many a believer has lost their faith because they were not fully prepared. As important as it is to carry the right equipment when embarking on a trip, equally important is what you choose to leave behind. Hebrews 12:1 (AMP) tells us to *strip off every unnecessary weight and the sin which so easily and cleverly entangles us, let us run with endurance and active persistence the race that is set before us."* Being prepared means letting go of anything that is heavy baggage; stuff that is only going to hinder us from moving in freedom towards our destiny .

What might God be identifying in your life that needs addressing? Perhaps it's self-limiting beliefs. I know I personally struggle in this area. Even as I work hard to finish writing this book, in the back of my mind, I'm thinking, "can I really publish this book? Do I have what it takes to market it?" So, what can I do to leave this kind of limiting thinking behind? Our thoughts can be our biggest enemy. Recognising the real enemy behind the way we think will help us to know how to deal with it. If you read your Bible, you'll know that the battle is spiritual rather than physical. *"For although we live in the natural realm, we don't wage a military campaign employing human weapons, using manipulation to achieve our aims. Instead, our spiritual weapons are energized with divine power to effectively dismantle the defences behind which people hide. We can demolish every deceptive fantasy that opposes God and breakthrough every arrogant attitude that is raised up in defiance of the true knowledge of God. We capture, like prisoners of war, every thought and insist that it bow in obedience to the Anointed One."* 2 Corinthians 10:3- 5 (TPT). What does this passage tell us? That we must capture any thoughts that are out of whack and bring them into alignment with God's truth. If we don't, our thoughts will manipulate and control us, holding us back from what we are created to be. When Satan tried it on with Jesus, He had to contend against Satan by speaking the truth out loud. As mentioned in a previous chapter, making declarations is a powerful weapon against the enemy. I don't believe that Satan and his minions are able to hear our thoughts, but I surely do believe they can influence them. In the desert, when Satan tempted Jesus to turn a stone into bread, did he read Christ's thoughts? Then how did he know that Jesus was hungry. Well duh! Jesus hadn't eaten for forty days. It doesn't take a genius to work that out. The enemy is very clever at reading the signs. He may not be able to read your thoughts, but he can read your body language. He can tell what you're probably thinking by what comes out of your mouth. That's why it's so important that we are careful with what we say. Thinking and speaking cause a chain reaction. If you think something, then sooner or later, it'll come out of your mouth. Likewise, if you say something, it will also impact your thoughts. It is difficult to control what we say if our thoughts are left unchecked. In Hebrews 12:1, we are advised to throw off what is hindering us, and as I have just been saying, our thoughts are one of those things. But verse 2, tells us to focus on Jesus. How do we focus on Him? By intentionally focusing our thoughts on who He is and what He has done for us. Like it says in Philippians 4:8. Think about what is good and true and lovely.

This is all part of allowing God to prepare us for the next season. In the chapter about perspective, I mentioned creating a vision board. What we set before our eyes is going to impact what we think about. Creating a vision board is a proactive way of focusing our thoughts on where we want to be rather than where we are. It focuses our thoughts on what we believe God has called us to, rather than our attention on our present circumstances—how things seem to be when nothing seems to be happening, or everything seems to be going wrong. Part of being prepared is having a clear vision. That doesn't always mean we know all the details about the future, or how it will come to pass. It's more that we know what lane we are in. Let me explain.

For most of my life, I have been searching for my purpose. I have lots of different creative interests and a heart to serve the Lord, but I never could work out where to focus my talents. It seemed like there were so many different things I could do, but I didn't want to just do anything. I wanted to do what God had called me to do. It wasn't until two years ago that I asked the Lord, "what is my vision?" I felt the Lord say that I am called specifically to women, to help them to be all that they can be in their identity in Christ Jesus. So now I know, what my vision is, and I know what lane to stay in. Whatever I do, I ask, "is this ministering to women, and is it helping them to be all they are called to be in Christ?" Obviously, I'm not talking about doing the housework, although even that helps me relate to other women to better understand them.

When an athlete is preparing for a big event, they spend many hours working on their strength, agility, and fitness. In 1 Timothy 4:7-8 (AMPC) it says... *"Train yourself toward godliness (piety), [keeping yourself spiritually fit]. For physical training is of some value (useful for a little), but godliness (spiritual training) is useful and of value in everything and in every way, for it holds promise for the present life and also for the life which is to come."* That's why it's so important that we embrace the in- between times, the times of waiting for what we dream about, when the vision is not yet fulfilled. That is the time to get spiritually fit and fully equipped for the future. Don't waste that precious time. IT IS A TIME TO PRESS INTO GOD. Enjoy those intimate moments in the secret place with the Father. Don't give up on your dreams just because they are delayed in coming. Surrender to the process. Allow God to prepare and transform you, empower and equip you to step into your destiny when the time is right.

So, how does the time of process protect us? God uses that time to prepare us, as I have just stated. The account of Noah in the bible is a great example of how preparation is the very thing that later protected Noah and his family from the flood. So how did Noah prepare? God had a plan. It wasn't Noah's plan. Noah had no idea what was even coming. He had no experience to draw from. He had to follow God's plan and do exactly as God instructed him without having any idea of what he was preparing for!! It takes complete obedience and faith to follow through as Noah did. Sometimes being prepared is simply doing what you know to do; simple obedience. To be obedient, you have to be close enough in relationship to God to know what He is instructing you to do in your unique set of circumstances. Part of being prepared is spending time with God in the 'secret place'. We have to be intimate enough to hear the still, small voice of God. He generally doesn't shout. Those in-between times are the perfect time to press into God and study the Word-fill ourselves with the truth so that it becomes ingrained in us. That's going to hold us in good stead when we are on the front lines; when we are actively moving in our calling.

To be honest, I feel a bit like Noah at the moment. I know something's coming, but I don't have a clear vision yet. I have to walk by faith, not by sight. In fact, I received a word of prophecy about it just this past Sunday. All I know is that God is moving me into something new that will impact others for the kingdom, something different that I have not experienced before, and that I won't be able to rely on the things I have relied on in the past to get me through. Unlike Noah, I have not had a voice from Heaven giving me detailed instructions on what steps to take moving forward. So how can I be obedient? I may not have heard an audible voice telling me what to do, but I have the word of God. I have the prophecies I have received, and I have the nudging of the Holy Spirit as I have spent time in God's presence in the 'secret place' seeking Him in prayer. I also have also received messages of confirmation and encouragement through dreams in the night that I have been able to interpret. He hasn't exactly spelt it out for me, but there are things I know to do, so it is wise for me to obey these promptings. Just briefly, in one of the dreams I had, I was in the back of a van. Something was obstructing my view. I felt caged in. However, the van was being driven by someone who symbolised Christ, and the van was still moving forward and in the right direction. I believe Holy Spirit was saying to me, "You may not be able to see where you're going—to see what's next, and you may be feeling constricted, but you are moving in the right direction even if it doesn't feel like it. Don't try to take the wheel. Take a back seat;

meaning let go of control. If you try to take the wheel, you will end up in the ditch." In order to obey, I have to surrender the need to know exactly what's coming, and I need to let go of control and just continue in a state of peace and trust, knowing that God's timing is perfect and He will bring it to pass when He judges best for me.

There's a saying, "if you ask God for something, then you need to get ready to receive it." Here's a practical example of how I did just that last year. I had asked God to provide the means for us to do a renovation on our garage, converting half of it into a TV lounge. Now, we were in the middle of a lockdown due to Covid 19, and at that time, there was no way we could get started on it. There were far too many restrictions. I could have sat back and gotten all glum about this, but instead, I acted in faith. I decided that I needed to prepare as best I could by firstly cleaning out the garage and secondly by starting to buy the doors and windows online while I was waiting. When I did eventually buy several materials, I had to make it clear that obviously, I would not be able to come and pick up the items until we came out of lockdown. When that day finally arrived, I was all set to get stuck into the renovation. The garage was already cleaned out, and the main materials had already been purchased. When waiting for a promise to be fulfilled, it is better to concentrate on what we can do rather than on what we cannot! Perhaps you would like to be a missionary in some far-off land. God may not have opened the door for you just yet, but in the meantime, could you start learning the language? Perhaps you and your spouse are longing to start a family. Nothing can truly prepare you for parenthood, but taking a parenting course or reading some good parenting books won't hurt. If you are truly serious about moving into a promise—pursuing a dream, you have to do something that looks foolish to the rest of the world. Noah is a perfect example of this. It doesn't actually say that Noah was mocked by the people who saw what he was doing, but can you imagine? It took over 100 years to build. Surely in that time, Noah would have questioned whether He had really heard from God. Surely people would have questioned what on earth he was doing and where was this huge flood that was supposedly coming? It can feel foolish to prepare for something that has not actually materialised. That's what faith is all about. Faith is getting ready; believing God has promised and that He will deliver. Faith without action is just phoney, as it says in James 2:17 in The Passion Translation.

So...confession time. Writing about this stuff is so much easier than actually putting it into practice. I've been doing well lately, feeling at peace and surrendering to the process, but I'm thinking this is too good to be true because, in the past, I would have been itching and agitated by now. Well, in the last couple of weeks, I have struggled to 'keep my faith on'. I have had a few wobbly days where I have felt a bit down, frustrated and anxious. Some days I feel like life is passing me by. I want to know what the future holds, and I want to get busy doing it. Why can't I just relax and enjoy this season of rest? How fortunate am I not to have to go out to work every day to earn a living? I'm trying to remain grateful and in a peaceful state of mind—I'm trying to appreciate every day as it comes, but the truth is, some days, I fail. God is so loving and kind. He understands that I'm struggling with feeling a lack of purpose lately. He knows that I am anxious to make the most of the summer days because winter is looming, and I struggle with the cold, darker days. So yesterday, God lovingly reminded me how fortunate I am to have good friends who will get me out of the house. I reached out to a friend at the beginning of the week and shared how I have been feeling of late. I asked her to check her schedule to see if she had time to spend with me because I knew it would help. She suggested we go out for a swim and perhaps a paddle. I bought a stand-up paddleboard last week because I knew I needed to try and get out of the house more and be a little more active. She invited another friend to come along with us. We spent the afternoon paddle boarding up a tidal river, followed by a nice swim. When we got back to the car, and I was packing up my paddleboard, I felt suddenly down in the dumps again. It just hit me all of a sudden, even though I had just had a fun time with my friends. They noticed me looking glum and asked if I would like to go back to their home for a swim in their pool and get ice cream on the way. I hesitated because I knew that it was getting late and I'd need to get home and get the dinner on soon. In the end, I said I'd go with them, and I'm so glad I did. We had a lovely time chatting together while enjoying a cold drink in the pool. Dinner was a bit later that night, but actually, it all worked out fine. Just as I finished eating my dinner, another friend turned up to take me for a nice bush-walk. I felt so much brighter after that. It's always good to have friends for support when you are struggling. Having a plan for those times when it seems like nothing is happening, is important. The enemy likes to attack when we are at our weak point. Gathering a network of supportive people around us that we can call on during these low times is essential to surviving the process. Part of preparing for the assignment that God has called us to is nurturing healthy relationships that will later be our support and encouragement when we eventually get the green light.

- David had his mighty men. *"For day by day men kept coming to David to help him, until there was a great army, like the army of God."* 1 Chronicles 12:22 (AMP)
- Ruth had Naomi: "But Ruth replied, *"Don't ask me to leave you and turn back. Wherever you go, I will go; wherever you live, I will live. Your people will be my people, and your God will be my God."* Ruth 1:16 (NLT). Although it was Ruth who went to support Naomi, ultimately, it was Ruth who went on to fulfil God's promise. The tables were turned, and Naomi then became the support person.
- Jesus had the twelve disciples. *"At daybreak, he called together all of his followers and selected twelve from among them, and he appointed them to be his apostles."* Luke 6:13 (TPT) Don't try to go it alone.

It has been a few weeks since I wrote the previous paragraph. In that time, I have had some clarity about what's next for me. Basically, I have realised that I am an artist. Until recently, I couldn't really say that out loud with any confidence. I already knew that God had told me to simply continue doing what I was doing, and He promised to fill in the details as I went along. I already had a plan to paint portraits of ten women of different ethnicity and turn them into a book along with selling the originals. The lightbulb moment was when I realised that I was indeed an artist and needed to not only acknowledge that but also focus my attention on that. The plan is to get my art studio up and running and start selling my creations. Along with completing and publishing this book by the end of the year, that would be plenty to keep me busy. For the past few weeks, I've been loving life and just getting on with it. BUT now begins the difficult part. The part where I have to extend myself beyond where I feel confident. That's where those relationships become so important. I can't do this alone. I need the support and encouragement of others who may have more confidence or experience in these areas that I am lacking. Even today, I begin to panic and feel overwhelmed with the thought of trying to publish and market my book. I feel so inadequate. I question whether anyone would even want to read it. The truth is this is not the first book I've written. I wrote one and uploaded it to Amazon Kindle years ago. Back then, I didn't have the confidence or the experience to do it properly. It's only due to the process I've been through in the interim that I now have the determination and hopefully the courage and know-how to see it through to completion properly this time. I've developed a lot more friends along the way too. Like-minded people who I know I can depend on to help me get the job done.

Embracing the process is never easy, but it is well worth doing. As each process unfolds; as I surrender more and more fully to the transforming power of the process, I can honestly say that I shine a little brighter as the diamond I am created to be. I have had people testify to this also. I'm not quite perfected, (I say with a chuckle), but I'm getting there. Through the reading of this book, I hope that you, too, will learn to embrace the necessary process that God wants to take you through to bring out your glorious shine!

A WORD FROM LISA

"Every word written in this book is shared from personal experience. I can honestly say that I am a better, stronger, wiser person today because of the process that God has taken me through. He saw the raw potential—a diamond in the rough, full of hopes and dreams but without the ability to obtain, nor the strength to sustain them. The process seemed so painful at the time but now I can look back and see the hand of God gently and patiently moulding me into a place of obedience. Surrender didn't come naturally to me I must say, but I am so glad that God didn't leave me in my undefined state. He is refining me to bring out my shine so that ultimately I may be a reflection of Him. He wants to do the same for you.

Contact Lisa

I would love to hear how you were impacted or inspired by reading this book. If you have any questions or you'd like me to pray with you concerning anything on your journey to 'shine like a diamond', please contact me by email at dewshq@gmail.com

You may like to check out some of my other creative projects at www.lisadewcreations.com

www.ingramcontent.com/pod-product-compliance
Lightning Source LLC
Chambersburg PA
CBHW022016290426
44109CB00015B/1188